To the Edge

To the Edge

❖ ❖ ❖

Reflections on Kingdom Leadership, Mission, and Innovation

J. D. Payne

Cover art by: Upper Air Creative
Author Photo: Jonathan Whitt

Unless otherwise noted, Scripture quotations are taken from THE ENGLISH STANDARD VERSION © 2001 by Crossway Bibles, a division of Good News Publishers.

ISBN: 1508511403
ISBN-13: 9781508511403

Other Books by J. D. Payne

Missional House Churches
The Barnabas Factors
Discovering Church Planting
Evangelism
Pressure Points
Kingdom Expressions
Strangers Next Door
Roland Allen
Apostolic Church Planting
Developing a Strategy for Missions (co-authored)
Missionary Methods (co-edited)

Free ebooks at jdpayne.org
Discipleship in Church Planting
Leading Your Church in Church Planting
Unreached Peoples, Least Reach Places

About the Author

J. D. Payne (Ph.D., The Southern Baptist Theological Seminary) is the pastor of church multiplication with The Church at Brook Hills in Birmingham, Alabama. He has served as a pastor with churches in Kentucky and Indiana, on church planting teams, and as a seminary professor. J. D. is the author of many books and articles. He is married to Sarah and has three children, Hannah, Rachel, and Joel.

When he is not looking for the best micro-roastery and espresso, he is considering how to become a pit master or a lead guitarist from the 1980s. He blogs at jdpayne.org and may be found on Twitter @jd_payne or contacted at jpayne@brookhills.org.

Acknowledgements

I want to thank Courtney Dziadul for her editorial assistance on this project. Much appreciation is due to Bette Smyth for proofreading this work, my assistant Jessica Giadrosich, Upper Air Creative for the cover design, and Jonathan Whitt for his photography skills.

I am also thankful for the elders, staff, and members of The Church at Brook Hills and for my family (Sarah, Hannah, Rachel, and Joel). Without these people, this book would not be what it is.

Much praise is to the Lord for His grace on this author and the production of this book.

To my Heavenly Father
and to my earthly partner, Sarah

Table of Contents

Preface

I have been blogging at Missiologically Thinking (jdpayne. org) for five years. From the beginning, my slogan for the site has been, *equipping the Church for the multiplication of disciples, leaders, and churches.* Each post has been written with this matter in mind. Over these few years, it has been a blessing to hear from my readers as they have shared words of encouragement, affirmation, challenges, and concerns related to the writings on the site.

To the Edge is a collection of several of those writings addressing matters of leadership, mission, and innovation. This book is written to inspire, encourage, exhort, provoke, challenge, and equip you for our Great Commission task. Hopefully, these writings will nudge—and even push—you *to the edge* where change happens. And change *must* happen. The four billion remain without Christ.

I can help you to the edge, but you are responsible for that all-important next step.

Before I finished writing this Preface, I took time to pray for those who would read this work. While we may never meet this side of heaven, I hope my prayer and these brief words may be of encouragement to you in your Kingdom efforts. Keep up the good fight!

J. D. Payne
Birmingham, Alabama
November 2014

Leadership

Saving the Crowds by Getting Away from Them

"But he would withdraw to desolate places and pray" (Luke 5:16).

Shocking words. Unbelievable words. I mean, how could He? He only had a ministry span of three years. Time was ticking. He knew this.

He had just healed a man with leprosy (v. 12-13). Word about Him had started to spread like wildfire. The crowds, great crowds, were coming, coming, coming and gathering around Him.

And for what reason? For hearing and for healing (v. 15). They wanted to hear what this miracle man had to say. Could He be a prophet? Is this the promised Messiah?

They wanted to be healed of "their infirmities."

And what was Jesus' response?

He would get alone with God.

Here was a great opportunity to share the gospel. Didn't He realize that? He said that was why He came

(Luke 4:18). Here was a great opportunity to give sight to the blind. He said He came to do that too (Luke 4:18).

Yes, He realized the importance of being there with the people; however, He realized there was a place of even greater importance. He would return to the crowds, having compassion on them. But now, even with the pressing crowds, it was more important to be in the desolate place.

If you are going to save the crowds, you must leave them for the One.

Lord willing, there will always be another opportunity to share the gospel, another sermon to preach. You will have another chance to heal people. There will always be another crowd to listen to you.

We will never be able to bear the fruit that our Father desires if we forget the source of our strength. It is out of relationship, not routine ministry, that we are able to do the works of Him who sent us while it is still day.

In your heart of hearts, would you rather be with the crowds or be in a desolate place alone with your Father? If your answer is the former, you may need to get to a desolate place today and talk with Him about your heart's desire.

❖ ❖ ❖

Too Glad for Gideons, Too Satisfied with Samsons

In our desire to see results happen in the Kingdom, we are often too thrilled to have the Gideons lead us. We are many times satisfied with Samsons.

If Gideon could defeat a huge army with only 300 men, we want someone like him as our leader! We want that kind of man for our team, to lead our organization, to pastor our church!

Samson could rip open a lion with his bare hands and kill 1000 men with a jawbone. We need someone like him to lead our team! What a track record. He can get 'er done!

And in our desire for such dynamic leaders, we lock arms with them and are willing to overlook their problems:

"And Gideon made an ephod. . . . And all Israel whored after it" (Judges 8:27).

"Samson went to Gaza, and there he saw a prostitute, and he went in to her" (Judges 16:1).

No leader is perfect. All are sinners; however, as long as we can have forty years of rest from the Midianites and twenty years of protection from the Philistines, we are often willing to compromise where we shouldn't.

Are you too glad for Gideons and too satisfied with Samsons?

Such is not the way of the wise Kingdom citizen on mission.

❖ ❖ ❖

The Real Deal or No Deal

Sociologist Erving Goffman drew from the theatrical metaphor when he helped us understand that life involves frontstage and backstage actions. The presentation of self in everyday life occurs differently when we are in public and around certain individuals (frontstage) and when we are alone or in private situations (backstage). The manager of a restaurant presents himself in one fashion to the customers and in another fashion when in the kitchen with the cooks. The CEO of a company manifests different characteristics in the boardroom than with the family.

While some changes in action and demeanor are expected and healthy, too much change in behavior as we move from the frontstage to the backstage is not healthy.

Over the past twenty years, I have had the opportunity to be with many Kingdom leaders as they functioned in both frontstage and backstage worlds. While there are many leaders who are authentic in their convictions, attitudes, and actions, unfortunately, I have also seen some leaders breakdown in character when they were backstage. What appeared to be a great frontstage presentation was not consistent with their backstage lifestyle. Continuity of character is important (Philippians 2:15).

Failure of character is the surest way to lose credibility in the eyes of those serving with you. And it is very difficult (if not impossible) to regain that trust once it is lost. The world may believe the frontstage performance, but those closest to you will know the truth and that will lead to a slow but devastating breakdown in the implementation of your strategy.

Consistency is critical!

If you are looking for leaders with whom to serve on a team, look for those who are the real deal both frontstage and backstage. Even more, as you are raising up leaders for making disciples of all nations, make sure *you* are the real deal both frontstage and backstage.

If you can't find such a team, it is better not to have one. A weak team will do more harm than good for the Kingdom.

If you have character flaws, work to eliminate them. Don't transfer those flaws to others who look up to you. There are too many inconsistent leaders out there already. And we know how our Lord describes those who honor Him with their lips, but their hearts and actions are far from Him. Apart from Him, we can do nothing (John 15:5). Spend time with Him and deal with your flaws immediately.

We are either the real deal or no deal at all.

❖ ❖ ❖

The Blight of Arrogance in the Field of the Kingdom

Arrogance is a blight in the Field of the Kingdom. Many struggle with it. Some of us privately. Some of us publicly. Unconfessed, it grows and consumes, grieves and quenches, and it always results in death. The individual may accomplish many great things while covered with this blight and gain the praise of many. But the Lord will not tolerate arrogance because it takes glory away from Him.

Knowledge puffs up. And so does missiology—our study of mission. Yet, the Lord calls us to walk humbly with Him, which includes the way we approach Him, His mission, His Church, and His world. We all have a missiology by which we live. But is it a humble one?

Among many things, a biblical missiology is humble, always willing to grow in understanding of God's truth and the application of means to the real world for the multiplication of disciples, leaders, and churches.

A biblical missiology is humble, clinging tenaciously to a scriptural foundation, holding tightly to principles, but loosely to strategy, methods, traditions, organization, and structures.

A biblical missiology is humble, focused and sure before arriving on the field, but allowing the Spirit and context to shape the application of never-changing truth.

A biblical missiology is humble, patiently and graciously bringing brothers and sisters along in the journey who have not been eating and drinking Kingdom-expanding concepts for as long as you have.

A biblical missiology is humble, knowing with confidence what it knows but open to correction and new directions.

I have observed a great deal of arrogance over the years in both my life and in the lives of many others. And we evangelicals seem to be okay with it as long as such people seem to be successful. But what will it ultimately profit us to make many Great Commission accomplishments in the name of the King only to have those successes rejected by the King? Remember, some people will do great things for the King, but He will deny knowing them (Matthew 7:21-23).

The Farmer is never okay with blight in His Field.

If we truly recognize that we are "unworthy servants" (Luke 17:10) on this journey, we must run to the Spirit to enable us to turn from that which so easily entangles us. We must plead for grace to embrace our great salvation, commission, other brothers and sisters, and the world with a contrite and broken spirit and a heart filled with love. We must move forward, wearing a towel instead of acting as if we are sporting a kingly robe.

May the Savior empower us and show us the way to live with a humble missiology in light of the four billion souls who do not know the Lord!

❖ ❖ ❖

Just Because It Works
It works! Let's do it!

This is a philosophy that often drives many churches, agencies, institutions, and networks; yet, we rarely state it this way. To do so, would mean that we embrace pragmatism.

Wow! Look at these results. Therefore, our means to the end justifies the outcome. Great results are not always of the Lord—consider the Mormon Church.

Over the years, I have been amazed at some theologically astute leaders who in public rail against pragmatism, but in private meetings they are willing to compromise to achieve a certain outcome.

Just because we can, doesn't mean we should.

Oh, I am not pushing against being practical, but against the willingness to embrace pragmatism when the going gets tough and all eyes are upon you for results. Wise Kingdom stewards are to be pragmatic to a degree; we are called to bear fruit and make disciples. We want to know what works; this is an element of the Kingdom Ethic. Pragmatism, however, is a philosophical view that results in bending core biblical values for the sake of supposedly godly gains. Externally, it may look like you haven't compromised on anything, but an internal assessment would tell a different tale.

When we walk closely with the Lord, He will make our paths straight (Proverbs 3:5-6).

But straight does not always mean high numbers, popularity, excitement, or that you will be invited to speak at great conferences.

Yes, but your path will be straight.

We need more leaders who are willing to walk the straight path of Christ instead of journeying along the compromising curves that provide many exciting accomplishments to put on a résumé. "The integrity of the upright guides them, but the crookedness of the treacherous destroys them" (Proverbs 11:3).

❖ ❖ ❖

Where the Buck Stops in the Kingdom

Teachers who offer models for learning basic subjects prepare their students for more advanced work. But sadly many teachers fail to properly teach the basics. This hinders the advancement of a culture and contributes to an impotent society. The next generation must be educated to continue the forward progress of a group. The buck is not to stop; it is to be passed on to others in replicable forms.

We may often feel that we are essential and unique and that the buck stops with us. After all, if we want something done right, we must do it ourselves. Who can do the best job? We can, of course!

However, we must understand that effective ministry is about equipping, empowering, and releasing others to possibly bigger and greater Kingdom endeavors.

Remember the words of our Lord, "Truly, truly, I say to you, whoever believes in me will also do the works that I do; and greater works than these will he do, because I am going to the Father" (John 14:12). It is amazing to me that those who would come after Jesus would do greater works than He did. Jesus was looking into the future and seeing all the wonderful Kingdom works of the generations after Him done in the power of the Holy Spirit.

One of my favorite quotes from Charles Brock comes from his book *Indigenous Church Planting.* Brock claims,

One man who is able to plant a church so modeled that very few ever could approximate his success is not thinking world evangelization. He is nearsighted. There may be room for unique models that are not reproducible, but if the world is to be reached, it will be by multiplication and not by addition.

True in church planting. True in all of ministry.

Does the buck stop with you? In the Kingdom's economy, the buck only stops on that Day.

And since that Day has not arrived, we better make sure we are passing the buck along.

❖ ❖ ❖

The Conference No One Hosts

"Leading this church through change was hard. I failed miserably many times; but here's what worked for us to grow from 50 to 500,000 in one weekend!"

"When we were planting our church, we did 1000 things wrong. I don't have time to tell you about those, so I'm going to tell you what did work!"

"Reaching this people group has been a blessing but very difficult. We made many mistakes, but you are here to hear what works."

No one schedules a conference called "The Things That Did Not Work."

No one would want to come to that. No one would flock to hear a bunch of people talk about the shortfalls. We would not pay for that. Plus, we are not secure enough in our identity in Christ to talk about our failures. That means being vulnerable, transparent.

We want to know what works.

Now, the reality is that often by the time we get to the "conference on stuff that works"—and definitely by the time we read the book—society has moved on. What was once on the cutting edge for that conference speaker is now five years removed from where society is (not to mention the contextual factors that were unique to them then and different for the rest of us now).

How about a gathering where little time passes between the execution of a strategy, its learned limitations, and when the strategist tells us of the limitations? Now that is a valuable gathering.

After hearing three or four people in the room share how in different ministry contexts each spent $25,000 but did not see much in terms of results, you would begin to reconsider spending your $25,000 on a similar project.

If there was a gathering of different people from different contexts addressing a common issue by talking about what is not working, that is a gathering I would be interested in. Knowing what is not currently working so well in the Kingdom is a stewardship matter.

Knowing what is working is not sufficient. Important? Yes! But, not sufficient. Zeal without knowledge is not wise; he who makes haste with his feet misses the way (Proverbs 19:2).

But don't expect such a conference soon.

❖ ❖ ❖

Mites, Breadcrumbs, and Kingdom Paradox

The Kingdom Ethic includes the following peculiar matters:

- Many who are first will be last, and the last first (Matthew 19:30).
- Everyone who exalts himself will be humbled; everyone who humbles himself will be exalted (Luke 14:11).
- Jesus came as a suffering Messiah.
- We are to be living sacrifices.
- If we want life, we must die to self.

What appear to be contradictions to us are actually major components of the Kingdom economy. Our Lord accomplishes His purposes in ways that are beyond our thoughts (Isaiah 55:8-9), even doing more than we can imagine (Ephesians 3:20).

Our Lord takes our limitations and uses them for His glory in gospel advancement. He is able to take our mites and multiply their value. Our few pieces of bread and small fish have exponential reach in His hands.

Over the past several years, I have observed this one peculiarity in gospel advancement that has received scant attention: Less is often more.

Although poverty does not guarantee that the Lord will be obliged to do great things with a person or group, we often do observe great advancements in missions among Kingdom citizens who have very little of this world's resources.

For historic examples beyond the first three centuries, we can turn to the early Moravians, Baptists, and Methodists on the American frontier. Today, we can observe similar work of the Spirit in many impoverished churches in Asia, Africa, and the Latin world.

But before we start to think that great advancements are directly related to few resources, we need to look beneath the surface. As I have observed contemporary groups and studied others in history, a common thread generally included the following:

1) They had a theological identity firmly rooted in the Word of God. They did not deny the truth of the Scriptures and understood who they were in Christ.

2) They had a driving zeal coming from their theological identity and believed that people without Jesus were separated from God and that only the gospel could transform lives, homes, and societies.

they had an apostolic focus. They understood that they were not commanded to make converts or plant churches. Rather, they were to make disciples of all nations, which involved intentional evangelism that resulted in churches being planted.

4) They had a biblical simplicity. Their resources, structures, traditions, and organizations did not get in the way of the mission. Such things were necessary and important, but they were not so complex that gospel advancement was sacrificed for the maintenance of a system.

We must remember that the Lord can use whatever He has put into our hands, be it great resources or mites and breadcrumbs.

The following questions are worth considering:

- Have we become so caught up in our blessings that we have lost our theological identity?
- Have we moved from our original missional focus?
- Have we "grown out of" our apostolic zeal, believing we are more sophisticated now?
- Have we moved so far away from biblical simplicity that we are now engrossed in having to spend most of our time, efforts, energy, and resources addressing issues and supporting structures that hinder the advancement of the gospel?
- Are we working hard to manage the good at the expense of maintaining the best?

If we find ourselves in an unhealthy situation, repentance is the beginning of the road to recovery. But while some changes are simple and quick, others will be painful and difficult. Our Father is gracious and is still on mission, empowering us to preach the gospel to all nations across the world and across the street.

❖ ❖ ❖

Breaking the Shock of the Obvious

What is obvious to you as a leader is not always obvious to others. Sometimes our familiarity with the obvious shocks us into silence. Being a wise steward with the wisdom and opportunity from the Lord often means overcoming this silence.

The temptation for many of us is that to us the obvious is so obvious that we tell ourselves, "I can't say anything about this matter. Everyone will think I am a poor leader. That is elementary. It is on everyone's mind. To open my mouth now and make such a simple statement of resolution would be a waste of time and leadership credit. It must be more complex."

But it is not always on everyone's mind. The solution is not always complex.

You know the wrench will fix the leaky faucet, but others do not, even those who often work with wrenches.

Part of excellence in leadership involves reminding people of the obvious. The effective leader is someone out in front. Leaders are ahead of others, farther down the path, at least a few steps.

Leaders walk where few others are walking. They think thoughts the majority are not thinking. They see things others often fail to see.

Leaders live in the world of the obvious so others can come to dwell there.

But sometimes leaders reside in that world for so long that they come to believe everyone lives there.

Solomon was once confronted with a conundrum that no one else was able to solve. He quickly resolved the matter with a solution obvious only to him (1 Kings 3:16-28), for the "wisdom of God was in him to do justice" (v. 28).

As the faucet continued to drip, Solomon saw the wrench nearby.

Maybe the matter is obvious to us because we are the Lord's leaders for the hour. Maybe the divine wisdom we have received requires us to speak and overcome the shock of silence.

Will people listen to your obvious solution? Yes. Maybe. Not always. Remember how the foolishness of ten spies triumphed over the wise direction of the two (Numbers 13)?

So, whenever a challenge comes along in your next meeting, take a leadership risk and state the obvious. Maybe someone will agree and see the wrench and fix that faucet that has been dripping for a few years.

Art for the River

We live in the age of the instant. We want to know what works and we want it now.

In our scientific and rationalistic world, we often attempt to make ministry a science. Such is not always the case. It is not that definite.

We co-labor with a dynamic Spirit. The unexpected is to be expected.

We co-labor with sinful people filled with the dynamic Spirit, but who are not robots that respond with 100% predictability. Remember the last time we said, "I can't believe he did that." "Wow! That is unbelievable!" "No way!" What should surprise us is our surprised reaction, not the person's action. Over the past twenty years, I have observed that even the most predictable people are unpredictable at times (sometimes for the good, sometimes for the bad).

While the Lord has established the channel in which the river of living water runs, those river banks are wide. There is much room for the unpredictable. The unexpected. The circumstances that cause us to adjust our strategies within the divine boundaries.

When we realize the nature of the task to which we are wonderfully called, we recognize that there is a great deal of art present. Even as we rightly call people to imitate us as we imitate Christ (1 Corinthians 11:1), we labor to lead them to the contextualization and application of biblical truth. This is an artistic expression. This should not surprise us, knowing the creativity of our Father. Even His Word is filled with poetry.

Art cannot be taught. Sure, we can teach the scientific aspects of painting—brush strokes, shading, depth, blending of colors, and texture. But the real art of painting comes when the student applies what has been taught to create a personal style.

Art cannot be taught. Sure, we can teach guitar students guitar science—triads, pentatonic scales, theory, improvisation, and shredding. But the real art of guitar comes when the student applies what has been taught and creates a personal style.

How are you equipping your people? In your church? Classroom? Small group? At home? Are you trying to program robots or note the divinely-set river banks and teach others how to apply biblical truth to the river of life? The former leader approaches ministry as a pure science; the latter recognizes the constants but understands the unpredictable. The former approach is fine with the generally predictable circumstance, but it freezes when confronted with many exceptions to the predictable. An automaton will always respond correctly in a select number of circumstances, but difficulties arise when real life happens.

And real life happens.

Equip. Don't program. Don't clone. Don't just teach the science.

Equip for application.

❖ ❖ ❖

Vowels of Service

The way we train others is often limited to a cognitive approach. This is most unfortunate. Such a model limits learning, retention, iteration, evaluation, and neglects a most vital aspect of learning–experience.

This limitation should not surprise us. We imitate what we know, and we know what has been modeled before us. In high school, college, and seminary, we became master notetakers. We know lecture is king in the domain of ministry preparation.

Thus, we carry this model with us to the local church. Knowledge is important, but knowledge is not everything.

A more comprehensive approach is needed for leading people to use their gifts for Kingdom service.

When equipping your people for the work of the ministry (Ephesians 4:11-12), give them the **Vowels of Service**. Your approach to preparing members of your church should include the following:

A = **Application** Provide them with hands-on opportunities to serve with the knowledge they receive.
E = **Education** Educate with a proper biblical/theological/missiological foundation.
I = **Inspiration** Inspire them with a biblical, God-sized, global vision.

O = Ownership Help them own the church's vision for the multiplication of disciples and churches.

U = Understanding Help them understand the global realities influencing the church and mission at home and abroad.

By engaging your people with the Vowels of Service, you are connecting with them at the three important levels for learning and life transformation: **Head** (education, understanding), **Heart** (inspiration, ownership), and **Hands** (application).

Know your Bible and teach it! Know your context. Use the Vowels of Service in your setting.

Break the model of the status quo; you know how far it has taken you and your church to date.

❖ ❖ ❖

A Marriage Made in Heaven

From time to time, I like to talk about my philosophy of theological education. I have taught in the classroom at the graduate and doctoral level full-time for ten years, plus an additional six years (and counting) part-time as an adjunct professor. I have spent a great deal of my life in the classroom in this capacity as well as in the role of a student.

My wife is a physician. I remember the long days of medical school followed by the even longer days of residency. My wife was not a doctor when she started medical school. And she was not allowed to go off on her own direction until she completed her residency training.

In North America a person is not legally allowed to practice medicine without the proper credentials. And in order to obtain the proper credentials, a person must pass through a set of predetermined standards that an accreditation board has established. To become a physician and be able to practice legally, individuals must complete college, medical school, and residency. Then they become grade A, 100% certified, physicians free to practice on their own (within the laws of the state and the US government).

Unfortunately, many people approach theological training much the same way as they understand medical training: go to school and let the academy certify that you are legitimate and ready.

A seminary does not make ministers of the gospel as a medical college makes physicians. My classes do not make missionaries or pastors. Sure, I can equip students for the ministry (Ephesians 4:11-12). But it is God who calls them. It is God who makes them. It is God who grows them.

While I'm obviously for a person obtaining as much theological education as the Lord would allow, no classroom is a substitute for field work. While in school, students should be significantly involved as leaders in local church ministry.

As I tell my students, the classroom is a sterile laboratory. It is a safe environment. In this controlled atmosphere, we are able to mine the depths of theological truths, wrestle with the application of missiological principles, and debate over missionary methods. This is a good thing.

But even the most practical discussions remain as theory until someone makes application. The gospel does not advance on theory alone.

My philosophy of theological education is deeply rooted in a marriage that I believe was made in heaven. This marriage sums up how all believers should be trained. This marriage is the union of the intellect with the application, the union of the mind with the hands. It is the union of the classroom-based training with the field-based training.

The intellectual component is never to be divorced from the practical component.

If theological education is not applied education for the edification of the Church, then it is of little value to the Kingdom. If the classroom does not play out on the field, then the classroom time is of little value in the multiplication of disciples, leaders, and churches.

In all of my courses I require field-based components. These components may consist of significant involvement with a church planting team, weekly field activities connected to a local church, observations, people-group research, serving with experienced church planters, or other brief field-based exercises.

Classroom-based and field-based training must be combined.

For what God has joined together to build Hi
I do not want to put asunder.

❖ ❖ ❖

Sincerity Is not Sufficiency

We have a heart for the lost.

We want to reach the unreached peoples living in North America and the rest of the world.

We need to be students of the Word.

We need to walk in step with the Spirit.

We have a heart for the poor.

Great! Sincerity is a start, but only a start. It is not sufficient to carry you through the race and across the finish line.

Convictions, passions, interests, and feelings are important. But what is your church, agency, or network doing to act on these desires. The psalmist writes, "The law of his God is in his heart; his steps do not slip" (Psalm 37:31), leading us to know that the righteous person (v. 30) is someone of both right desire and right action.

<u>If we sat down and had a conversation with your strategy, calendar, budget, and weekly activities, what would they say?</u>

Sufficiency needs sincerity. Just don't be fooled into thinking that sincerity is sufficiency. The four billion remain. The Day approaches.

❖ ❖ ❖

Missional Living in a Complex World – Part 1

Even though numerous books have been written on the topic of "missional" since the late 1990s, much confusion remains. I recently spoke at a conference in Missouri on the topic of missional living. During that time I attempted to answer some questions to cut through the fog of confusion. I've heard questions such as, "Is this 'missional stuff' something new?", "What is missional living?", "Can I live missionally today?" In these next two sections, I'll share with you some of what I presented.

NOT ROCKET SCIENCE

Missional living is not rocket science. When we look at the great number of discussions and writings about missional living, it is easy to assume that it is a difficult matter to understand and close to impossible to live out in our world today. Such is certainly not the case. Now, while I'm all for such discussions and publications (I've been a contributor to this conversation.), the reality is that missional living is nothing new for the church.

MISSIONAL LIVING OCCURS . . .

Missional living occurs when Kingdom citizens live according to the Kingdom Ethic in the world. People enter the Kingdom though the confession that Jesus is Messiah (Matthew 16:13-19) and are to live according to the standard of the King. His Ethic transcends the ethics of the kingdoms of this world. For example, "You have heard it said, 'do not commit adultery,' but I tell you . . ."; "You have heard it said, 'do not murder,' but I tell you . . ."; "The rulers of this world lord it over their subjects, but the first is to be last . . ."; "Who is greatest in the Kingdom? Take a look at these little children here . . ."

The Kingdom Ethic is the standard by which Kingdom citizens are to live in relation to God (Matthew 22:37-40), to other Kingdom citizens (Matthew 18:15-20), and to those who are outside of the Kingdom (Matthew 28:18-20). Packed into this divine rule is what we find throughout the Scriptures. As a Kingdom citizen, we do not have the option to relate to God on our own terms or desires. There are appropriate guidelines by which we engage with other brothers and sisters. This rule instructs us concerning how to interact with those who have never confessed Christ as Lord.

And while this Ethic is to be lived out in covenant with other Kingdom citizens in what is understood to be Kingdom communities (local churches), missional living is specifically directed toward the relationships with those outside of the Kingdom.

(A note is needed here. While space will not permit me to address the comprehensive nature of the other two relationships related to Kingdom living, it is important to understand that a breakdown in fellowship in these other two areas hinders missional living. When Kingdom citizens walk out of fellowship with God and with other brothers and sisters, global disciple making is hindered. When the Spirit of God is grieved, Kingdom expansion is affected.)

MISSIONAL LIVING REQUIRES . . .

Both actions and words are requirements for missional living. Kingdom citizens are to let their lights shine before men that they may see the good works and praise the Father who is in heaven. But Kingdom citizens must also preach the gospel in season and out of season. We cannot do one without the other. While some situations will require that we spend most of the time living out the Kingdom Ethic before unbelievers (1 Peter 3:1-2), we must proclaim the gospel. Without the sharing of repentance toward God and faith in the Lord Jesus (Acts 20:21), no one will be saved. Other situations will require more time spent on our words. Peter's encounter with Cornelius is an example of this. And while Peter spent most of his time preaching, his loving actions as a Jewish man being willing to enter into the home of a Gentile communicated the nature of the Kingdom Ethic (Acts 10).

❖ ❖ ❖

Missional Living in a Complex World – Part 2

The Bible should be our guide in matters of both belief and practice. The topic of missional living is no exception to this matter. While we could examine numerous passages that provide guidance for missional living, Colossians 4:2-6 offers six principles that we should embrace.

MISSIONAL LIVING MUST BE DONE PRAYERFULLY (3B)

We need to pray for opportunities to connect with people and share the gospel with them. Paul desired prayer for such opportunities. We must also trust in God to open such doors for the message. We need to pray for opportunities, words to speak, and for open hearts to the good news.

MISSIONAL LIVING MUST BE DONE WITH GOSPEL CLARITY (3C-4)

The mystery of the gospel has been revealed; now we must clearly communicate such truth to others. Our language (and actions) must be understood. We are to watch our language and constantly be asking, "How are they 'hearing' what I am communicating by my words and deeds?"

MISSIONAL LIVING MUST BE DONE WISELY (5A)

Literally, we are "in wisdom, to be walking." This walk is our lifestyle. Do we live wisely in relation to those outside the Kingdom? Unfortunately, many people today are not interested in Jesus because they know some of His followers. Are our lives reflecting the Kingdom Ethic, or do we manifest the ethics of another kingdom?

MISSIONAL LIVING MUST BE DONE INTENTIONALLY (5A-B)

We must go throughout our day with "Great Commission Eyes." A great evangelist of yesteryear once stated, "When I meet new people, I always see an 'L' or an 'S' on their foreheads. The 'L' stands for 'lost' and the 'S' stands for 'saved'. I assume that everyone has an 'L' until I know for certain that they are followers of Jesus." This is a good practice for us to follow. Missional living does not just happen. We must be intentional about it. We must be intentional about gospel engagement.

MISSIONAL LIVING MUST BE DONE GRACIOUSLY (6A)

Paul notes that our speech should always be gracious and seasoned with salt. Whenever people encounter us, do they see grace or a grouch? Humility or a hypocrite? Joy or a jerk? Love or a liar? 1 Peter 3:15-16 is a great verse to memorize.

MISSIONAL LIVING MUST BE DONE FLEXIBLY (6B)

The never-changing gospel must be communicated in ever-changing situations. Paul writes that we should know how to answer each person. This means that a customized approach is necessary when it comes to sharing the gospel. We must be students of God's Word, and we must be ready to respond appropriately to others.

Obedience is not a complicated matter. As I mentioned before, missional living is not rocket science. So, let's take off our white lab coats, put away our scientific calculators, stop analyzing and debating the trajectories as to who gets to go to the moon, and start living out the calling we have received.

❖ ❖ ❖

Loving without the Act

I love to talk about evangelism, sharing our faith, and going to the nations.

I love hearing my pastor preach. "Preach it, brother!"

It is great that we have the poor on our hearts.

I love God.

Are you in love with the idea? The concept? The experience? The argument? The discussion? If so, then the one who is in love is one who acts on that love.

Jesus said, "If you love me, you will keep my commandments" (John 14:15). James wrote, "Faith apart from works is useless" (James 2:20).

So...

What if we examine our lives and find no action related to that which we claim to love? Only talk. Debate.
Little obedience.

Maybe we are not really in love after all

❖ ❖ ❖

Theology, the Last Resort

It was tragic that the building was destroyed. "What are
you and the church going to do now," the reporter asks
the pastor.

"We will carry on. The church is the people, not the
building."

The atmosphere of the meeting was solemn but joy-
ful. "Our agency does not have the money to send more
people. So, let's consider sending tent makers."

"I'm needing some wisdom on this serious matter. I
need to spend some quality time with the Lord—maybe
even fast."

"He is getting very old; he even had a stroke six months
ago. I need to share the gospel with him."

"Retirement begins next year. I think I will consider taking the gospel to other nations, now that I have
time."

It is troubling that we often become more biblical when
the difficult realities of life occur, our possessions are removed, and the comfort is gone. We get theologically serious.

What would happen if we allowed biblical doctrine to guide our lives each day, every day?

Let's stop using theology as our last resort.

"Teach me good judgment and knowledge, for I believe in your commandments" (Psalm 119:66).

❖ ❖ ❖

Clanging or Fitly

How you say what you say is almost as important as what you say. Your medium matters.

You may be right and speak the truth, but your message is tainted because of your attitude.

You may be right and speak the truth, but your lifestyle behind closed doors contradicts your message.

Over the years I have been asked, "What do you think about what _____ said?" And often, over the years my response has been, "I agree with _____ 100%, but not with the demeanor in which he chose to speak."

"If I speak in the tongues of men and of angels, but have not love, I am a noisy gong or clanging cymbal" (1 Corinthians 13:1).

No more noise. No more clanging.

"A word fitly spoken is like apples of gold in a setting of silver" (Proverbs 25:11).

Be more fitly.

The world is watching and listening. The Church is watching and listening. A younger generation is watching the what and how of your model—and they'll reproduce it.

You may be right and speak the truth, but what I hear does not look like gold set in silver.

❖ ❖ ❖

Faithful Doing When You Don't Know What to Do

What do we do when we don't know what to do?

This is a question we ask often.

"I am fasting, praying, reading the Word, seeking wisdom in a multitude of counselors, but I am still not certain what to do."

Great! Keep up such practices! Such are wonderful disciplines of disciples!

"Yes, but how should I act in my situation? What should I do?"

Do something . . . something different.

While there are times the Lord wants us to wait in Jerusalem until the Spirit arrives (Acts 1:4), there are numerous situations that require immediate movement. Such is a matter of being a good steward. Leaders must be movers.

To bury your talent is to remain frozen, and to invest it is movement. It is faithful doing.

No, we do not continue to repeat the past that is not working, hoping that one day it will work. We learn from our past and then do a variation on it. We commit our ways to the Lord and then take a step of faith as we walk filled with the Spirit.

Remember the legend of Edison—10,000 tries before the light bulb worked to his satisfaction. How many tries do you think it took before they were able to develop these new energy-saving "green" bulbs?

Remember Paul? His church planting team tried to enter two different areas to preach the gospel, but they were interrupted by God (Acts 16). The result? The Philippian Church was planted, and we now have the book of Philippians. It was in the act of faithful doing that the Lord led the team according to His will.

Analyze for a season, but don't let it paralyze you. If you are looking for the perfect solution or the perfect route, stop looking. You will never find it. As long as we sinful beings are involved, it will never be perfect.

Die to self each day. Walk with God. And when you don't know what to do, faithfully do something for His glory. Act. Move on mission. He is able to get you to Philippi!

❖ ❖ ❖

Reproducing What We Know

We reproduce what we know. And, we know what is modeled before us.

If such is the case, then what happens when what we know is not accomplishing what needs to be done? We end up repeating ourselves, doing the same things with a slightly different variation while expecting new results to occur.

Such is not the way of the wise kingdom steward. The Kingdom Ethic demands more from us.

Whenever something systemically new comes along, it is initially viewed as inferior to the norm. It is not what is expected according to our structures. It often does not fit within our known models. It does not produce the expected results.

But if we reproduce what we know, yet we know that what is modeled before us is not working, then maybe it is time for something systemically different.

❖ ❖ ❖

When the Ordinary Does the Extraordinary

We want to start with the extraordinary. Iron Man. The Incredible Hulk.

"We want the high caliber, high capacity-type to lead this ministry. For apart from these we can do nothing. We want Superman, not the Greatest American Hero!"

We want to use the extraordinary to reach the world.

"If only our church had some outstanding leaders, then we would be better poised to reach the four billion. Unfortunately, global disciple making will have to wait until we can find just one."

We want the extraordinary because we think they are the way to accomplish the extraordinary.

"Kingdom work is a daunting task, please send us some strong leaders to enable our church to be about such work."

But . . . what if the way to reach the nations is not through the extraordinary? What if in our Father's Kingdom economy the primary way to accomplish the extraordinary is through the ordinary?

"Now when they saw the boldness of Peter and John, and perceived that they were uneducated, common men, they were astonished. And they recognized that they had been with Jesus" (Acts 4:13).

Do you catch that? The ordinary doing the extraordinary.

Yes, our Father uses the extraordinary to accomplish the extraordinary but not in the way we have come to believe. For the extraordinary is found in Jesus and not His followers' intellect, leadership capacity, experience, degrees, or charisma.

What about your church? Do you have any members who are common, ordinary people? Are you an ordinary person? If so, then you and your church are in a good position for the Lord to do the extraordinary through you.

"But ordinary people can't engage in extraordinary Kingdom work!"

Really? What is your definition of extraordinary?

"With all that they have going on with work and family, they can't organize, administrate, lead, preach, and conduct church ministries like I do."

Then maybe you need to revise your understanding of what is necessary for a healthy local church to exist and be involved in our Commission?

The way to accomplish the extraordinary is through the ordinary. The ordinary disciples of Jesus confounded the religious leaders of the first century. These ordinary men were accused of turning the world upside down (Acts 17:6). These ordinary people were responsible for the Word of the Lord going forth everywhere (1 Thessalonians 1:8).

And it was through the service of the ordinary that you and I eventually came to faith in the Extraordinary.

Stop looking for the extraordinary among people. Look for the ordinary who are filled with the Extraordinary . . . if you want to accomplish the extraordinary.

❖ ❖ ❖

Remembering the @

Imagine life without the ubiquitous @.

It is not hard to do if you can think back to the late 80s and early 90s. Twitter did not exist, and email was scarce.

Oh sure, only the accountants of the world were familiar with that symbol. They used it as an abbreviation for "at the rate of."

To the rest of the world, however, it was just a funny-looking lowercase a. No significance. No name. No credibility. Wasted space on the keyboard.

But now the @ is a necessary part of our daily lives. Even beyond email and Twitter, the @ has become accepted shorthand in normal conversation (e.g., Meet me @ the coffee shop.) Could we spend even one day without seeing or using the "shift + 2" keys on our computers or smart phones? No. The wheels of our daily grind would screech to a halt!

As we labor to raise up leaders, I can't help but wonder if we often treat some people like they are the pre-1990s @, not realizing their future Kingdom potential.

That guy will never be able to lead others well.

There is no way she has what it takes.

This person is a waste of my time.

I have had the great honor of training many church leaders over the years. I must confess at times I have looked at some people and thought, "No way," only later to see them prove to be very effective on the mission field or in established churches.

Forgive me, Lord.

Yes, we must use much wisdom, discernment, responsibility, community, and the testing of others as leaders. The Scriptures are clear that we should not be hasty when it comes to putting leaders in place. But we cannot determine leaders by looking only at their outward manifestations. When we are quick to judge by the externals, we fail to be guided by the Spirit of Christ.

Aren't you glad Samuel killed his flesh in this area and was led by the Spirit to find the leader from whom the Messiah would come (1 Samuel 16:7)? Let's trust our Father in the process of leadership development and follow His Spirit. He will make matters clear regarding the roles of such saints in His Kingdom.

If we are quick to judge odd and seemingly insignificant keys, then we will miss wonderful opportunities to equip and send a multitude of @'s.

❖ ❖ ❖

Hearing through the Complexity

I received a bittersweet compliment the other day: "I've been involved in church planting and always thought it had to be complex and complicated, but then I read your book *Discovering Church Planting* and realized that it can be simple." While I was honored and deeply appreciated this encouraging word, I am troubled that such a paradigm shift had to occur.

If the first-century disciples approached church planting with the complexity we have in North America, the gospel would have never left the Middle East.

There is little room at the church planting table for anything simple. We fail to remember the complex King we serve operates through some very simple means.

Now, while my encounter revolved around the topic of church planting, I can't help but wonder if we have in many ways made following Jesus into something that is very complex.

Do the biblical parameters allow for ecclesiological complexity in the Kingdom? Yes, in certain situations; however, we must also recognize that the Kingdom Ethic requires us to be wise stewards with our Christian freedom.

And in light of the four billion who have yet to call upon the name of the Lord, I often wonder if our cultural complexity hinders many unreached peoples from hearing—because many Christians fail to go, due to the complex channels.

❖ ❖ ❖

Our Practical Oxymorons

"I preach a simple gospel, but disciple making is very complex."

"I support our missionaries, as long as they are pastors."

"I want to see more people on the field, but must restrict the flow so only the high-capacity, one-man-band, charismatic leaders get there."

"I believe the local church is all we need for Christ's work, as long as we can get the parachurch to help us."

We like our practical oxymorons. They are terribly good. Oh, to give them up would be bittersweet.

Mission

Preparing for Nuclear War by Sharpening Our Arrows

If the cultural revolutions of our age are unprecedented, we should not be surprised that what is needed is a systemic missiological shift. Not a theological shift from "the faith that was once for all delivered to the saints" (Jude 3), but a return to a more apostolic approach for local and global disciple making, while ministering in areas of the Western world where a mature Church exists.

When I wrote *Pressure Points: Twelve Global Issues Shaping the Face of the Church*, I felt led to include a chapter entitled "West as a Mission Field." This is one global issue that will shape the face of the Church for the rest of our lives. Political, religious, ethnic, demographic, and cultural shifts have brought about such a change. Certain parts of the Western world are feeling these revolutions differently than others. Though the United States used to be several years behind Western Europe in this transition, we are quickly catching up.

More of what we have been doing when it comes to disciple making and church planting is not sufficient. More theological training like what we (in the West) have been doing for five centuries is not sufficient. To continue our present course, even in light of what most Americans are calling cutting-edge training and church planting, is not sufficient. Over the past thirty years, even the most progressive evangelical disciple making and church planting paradigms are slight variations on the status quo. A systemic shift is needed with our structures, organizations, training, and missionary practices.

To remain on the present path is like preparing for nuclear war by teaching our troops how to sharpen arrows for their bows.

Are bows and arrows still needed? Yes, for short-range combat that is likely to occur in any war. But if we are putting most of our convictions, resources, and energies into stockpiling arrowheads and rawhide strings, then we will be surprised.

Revolutions happen, and sometimes they happen quickly. Evangelicals are the utmost conservatives when it comes to philosophical and methodological change.

The war has started. And the enemy is not using bows and arrows.

When a Biblical Model is Viewed as Unusual

I recently spoke with a missions leader for a particular denomination. As we talked over coffee, he inquired about the direction of our church when it comes to church planting. My response was to describe our future missionary labors in terms of Acts 13-14; 16; 20; 1 Thessalonians 1:2-10; and Titus 1:5. He responded with much surprise, as if my thoughts were coming from an unusual source.

Unfortunately, over the years, I have found myself surprising many people during similar conversations.

What does it reveal about our missiology and biblical convictions when we think it is strange to advocate that those first-century church planting teams have something to teach us? What does it reveal about our Kingdom stewardship when we view such advocates as being peculiar? Do we not recognize that a problem exists when we label a church planter as being innovative, creative, or unusual for following a Pauline model?

Granted, not everything we read in the Bible is prescriptive; however, I believe our brother Paul and his example should be on a pedestal for us to consider. He was a church planter, you know.

As wise stewards of the mystery of Christ, we must subscribe to a definition of biblical church planting as evangelism that results in new churches. Or, to communicate it in other terms: disciple making that results in new churches. The weight of the biblical model is on this definition.

Imagine what would happen if we began to create a church planting atmosphere in North America in which the expectation for new churches is that they should consist of 100% new believers–at the moment those churches are planted.

Consider what would happen if our strategies did not embrace methods that would result in new churches forming primarily through the shifting of the saints around in the Kingdom.

What would happen if we recognized that a wise use of our Father's resources (e.g., money and people) should be to assist in planting churches out of the harvest fields, instead of establishing a new work in a community to provide a different style of worship/ministry for the believers who are already there—and to do evangelism, of course?

We do not need another flavor of church in the Baskin Robbins of North American Christianity; we need missionary bands to settle for nothing less than disciple making that results in new churches.

What would happen if we equipped and commissioned missionaries with the task of only going to the lost in the people group/community?

We say we want to see churches planted out of the harvest, but our actions and our leadership practices often do not match our words. And the sad thing is that even when faced with such inconsistencies, we are likely to continue repeating our past behaviors–expecting different results.

Whenever a biblical model for church planting is viewed as unusual, the path to change will come with pain.

In order for healthy change to occur, we have to change our ecclesiologies, missiologies, and what we celebrate, reward, and expect.

We have a poor understanding of our Commission. We act as if Jesus has commanded us to plant churches. We are commanded to make disciples. It is out of disciple making that churches are to be birthed. The weight of the biblical model rests here. Not on transferring growth. Not on acrimonious splits. It is evangelism that results in disciples, who covenant together to be and function as the local expression of the Body of Christ.

We have a poor understanding of the local church. If our definition is poor, then everything we say and do related to church planting will be poor. We often expect newly planted churches to manifest structures and organizations like what is observed in churches of 20, 40, 50 years of age. Our definition of a local church is often so encased in our cultural desires that we do not know the difference between biblical prescriptions and American preferences.

We operate from a poor definition of a church planter. If we do not recognize the missionary nature (and thus, apostolic functions) of church planters, we end up equating them with pastors. And take it from a pastor who has been involved in church planting: Missionaries and pastors have different callings, gift-mixes, passions, and functions to give to the Kingdom. We end up sending pastors to do apostolic-type work or sending missionaries to do pastoral work. These are perfect storms for problems, frustrations, burnout, and disasters.

Are there other ways to plant churches than what we read about in the ministry of Paul? Yes, and I am in favor of some of those models. Are there times when a church should hive-off members to begin work in another area? Yes. Is it okay for a congregation to send out a pastor with several church members to plant an "instant" church in a community? Yes, under certain circumstances.

However, such models tend to be difficult to reproduce (in view of four billion unbelievers), pose contextualization challenges, are costly, and often do not result in a great amount of disciples made. The weight of the biblical definition for church planting is not found here. Such models should be the exception when it comes to church planting. Today, they are often the expectation.

I expect my "surprising" conversations will continue in the future. Such is necessary as we move in a direction where a biblical model is not looked upon as the exception. But until our church planting expectations change, we must ask ourselves a question and recognize the troubling answer:

What do we have whenever a biblical mo
as unusual?

We have a major problem.

❖ ❖ ❖

Missiology of the Moment

The missiology necessary to advance the gospel in a post-Christianized context is not the same as the missiology that brought us to a Christianized context. Certainly, this does not mean a complete overhaul, but rather a building upon that which has gone before.

Some things must change while we return to an apostolic paradigm; however, one challenge is that we lack the vision for such an approach in view of a mature Church in the United States and Canada. And lacking this vision, we often fail to change that which truly must shift. We end up failing to ask the right questions.

A post-Christianized context is unlike a context where there is little to no gospel presence. A well-established Church exists with well-developed structures, organizations, and traditions. Yet, the multiplication of disciples, churches, and leaders requires an apostolic model. As it stands (and this is coming from a pastor), we are attempting to reach a context with pastoral approaches when missionary activity is required.

Even when we attempt such apostolic labors, we define them in pastoral terms and attempt to execute them through pastoral paradigms. This is not wise. For example, look at how we define church planting, and compare that with the New Testament.

What got us here is not sufficient for where we need to go. The wise Kingdom steward recognizes this and adjusts accordingly.

But that adjustment is difficult. It's easier to stick with the missiology of the moment.

❖ ❖ ❖

Asking for a Story

We love stories. We want stories. Without a story, we don't move.

I recently heard of two pastors locked in conversation. One shared with the other his thoughts on multiplying disciples and churches. His ideas were biblical and simple but did not fit the traditional paradigm. The other pastor replied, "You do it first and get a success story under your belt, then my church will do it."

Story. Give me a story, then I'll move forward. Tell me a story, then I'll consider it.

Peter didn't say, "Tell me a story to reach the God-fearers, and I'll try it." Sometimes you must be the first to go to Cornelius's house.

The unnamed men of Acts 11:19-21 didn't say, "Tell us a success story of what works to reach the Gentiles, then we'll preach the gospel in Antioch." Sometimes you must be the first to plant the Church in that city.

Stories. Give us a success story, then we'll push in when we know it is safe.

Safety and the American definition of success are never guaranteed in the Kingdom. Don't expect it!

Is there a place for wisdom and stewardship in Kingdom advancement?

Absolutely! But, that's different from refraining to move in a more excellent way until you have a success story.

What if William Carey had waited for a success story?

What if David Brainerd had required a success story before going to the Native Americans?

What if Ralph Winter had required a success story before talking about going to the hidden peoples (i.e., unreached peoples), and Luis Bush, before emphasizing the 10/40 Window?

Stop asking for a sign, a story of success, before being willing to try something new.

Someone has to be the first. How about you and your church?

❖ ❖ ❖

The West as a Mission Field

Though many of the Western nations of the world have historically experienced a strong Christian presence, the West is now a post-Christianized mission field. It was during the 200 years of the great advancement of the Protestant missionary movement that the ideologies of secularism, modernity, and postmodernity developed with much force. These helped facilitate the demise of Christendom. As time progressed, the shadow of the steeple shrank across the West and the chime of church bells grew faint. Western European contexts, once bastions for theological orthodoxy and missionary movement, are now spiritual deserts with only a small percentage of evangelicals.

While there are followers of Jesus who would not consider themselves evangelicals, researchers often use evangelical percentages to estimate the number of Christ-followers across the world. While there are certainly limitations to this benchmark, evangelicals clearly identify themselves (along with other matters) as those who have been born again as the required means for being a follower of Jesus and having a home in Heaven. Here are the nationwide evangelical percentages across a few Western countries:

- United Kingdom 9%
- Canada 8%
- Australia 14%
- New Zealand 18%
- Denmark 4%
- Netherlands 4%
- Switzerland 4%
- Germany 2%
- Spain 1%
- France 1%

And while the United States remains with a 26% evangelical presence, it also finds itself as a post-Christianized mission field. Even though states such as Alabama, Oklahoma, and Mississippi are comprised of about 40% evangelicals, this is clearly not the case across the country. Look at the following percentages:

- Utah 2%
- Rhode Island 2.5%
- Massachusetts 3%
- New Hampshire 4%
- Vermont 4%
- New Jersey 4%
- Connecticut 4%
- Maine 4.5%
- New York 4.5%
- Delaware 7%

And when we become even more specific, we see the following realities in some of our metropolitan areas:

- Provo-Orem, UT 0.5%
- Pittsfield, MA 2%
- Salt Lake City, UT 3%
- Utica-Rome, NY 4%
- Kingston, NY 2%
- Protland-Biddeford, ME 4%

A 2012 study confirmed that the US is no longer a Protestant-majority country. Adherents have dropped just below 50% for the first time. Coupled with this shift in Protestant numbers is the rise of Americans stating they have no religious affiliation. Presently, 20% of all US adults (thirty-three million) comprise the quickly growing category of the "nones." In all likelihood these demographic shifts reflect changes to come. Like the inching of a glacier that ever so slowly reshapes the land, changing faith systems are part of an ongoing sculpting process in the US. The country has now reached a tipping point in the numbers of those with little or no connection to a Judeo-Christian worldview.

The West is also a major recipient of large numbers of migrating Muslims, Hindus, Buddhists, and Atheists. The West is home to an estimated 1200 unreached people groups, with many of these representing some of the world's unengaged-unreached peoples.

❖ ❖ ❖

Returning to the Apostolic

Effective mission in the West is going to require the Church to return to a radically biblical approach to her labors. This return will cause many people to believe they have discovered something new, avant-garde, innovative, or creative. Nothing could be further from the truth. We need to frequent that which is already in place.

The challenge for the Church in the West is not just how to think about her context as a missionary should think but also how to act as a missionary would act in the shadow of dominant structures and organizations that are more pastoral in nature, birthed and developed within a Christian context of yesteryear.

The return to apostolic or missionary thought and practice will be a great challenge for many churches. If the late twentieth century brought about "worship wars" among congregations, I can only speculate how such missional shifts will be received. In light of how poorly we (at least, in the US) resist change, I believe few churches will make the necessary changes to reach the post-Christian West. Churches that are most likely to move forward effectively are those that embrace a radically biblical approach to sending missionary teams to function in apostolic ways when it comes to making disciples, planting churches, and appointing pastors in those churches.

❖ ❖ ❖

Missions Today: Learning from the Rest

In great areas of Asia, Africa, and Oceania, the church grows steadily and even spectacularly. But in the areas dominated by modern Western culture (whether in its capitalist or socialist political expression) the church is shrinking and the gospel appears to fall on deaf ears.

> *It would seem, therefore, that there is no higher priority for the research work of missiologists than to ask the question of what would be involved in a genuinely missionary encounter between the gospel and this modern Western culture. Or, to put the matter in a slightly different way, can the experience of missionaries in the cross-cultural transmission of the gospel and the work of theologians who have worked on the question of gospel and culture within the limits of our modern Western culture be usefully brought together to throw light on the central issue I have posed?* (Lesslie Newbigin, *Foolishness to the Greeks*, 3)

In the late 1990s, I had significant interactions with individuals who served as missionaries in countries other than the United States. During that time, I came to believe that the Church in the West could learn a great deal from those who had labored to advance the gospel in the non-Western world. Believing there was much for North Americans to learn from those serving "overseas," I wrote my doctoral dissertation (in 2001) on this subject.

It was during those days as a pastor and a doctoral student that I came to recognize that many other brothers and sisters (much wiser and more experienced than I) had been thinking along similar lines—for several decades. In fact, I soon realized they had written articles and books on the topic and even created a network to assist churches in the West to engage their contexts as missionaries.

Though Newbigin wrote about such missionary encounters in the West several years ago (his book quoted above was published in 1984), there still remains a great deal of change necessary for the development of a robust missionary encounter with those living in the West. We in North America have felt Newbigin's influence and have experienced the Missional Church Movement, both of which have lead us more in the direction of "a genuinely missionary encounter between the gospel and this modern Western culture." However, we remain well behind where we should be in our missionary thinking and work.

Brothers and sisters across the globe have assisted us in thinking about the United States in relation to missionary matters, such as understanding cultures, interpersonal communication, contextualization, and church planting. And in light of these recent adjustments to our approaches, we have experienced some healthy gospel advancement; however, certain systemic shifts (e.g., ecclesiological, strategic, and methodological), conducive to the multiplication of biblically faithful disciples, leaders, and churches across the third largest country in the world, are still necessary. Many of our activities still reflect missiologies that result in the development of structures, strategies, and methods that approach our contexts as if they are already reached, rather than resulting in activities geared for gospel engagement within highly diverse, globalized, post-Christianized, post-industrialized contexts.

Are we in the West learning from the rest? Yes. But, we are learning slowly—much, much too slowly.

❖ ❖ ❖

Apostolic Missiology—Part 1

I recently spoke to church planters at an event held in Atlanta by an evangelical mission agency. The main point I shared was this: In any context, the Church must operate from an apostolic missiology when it comes to missionary endeavors. Nowhere is this matter more urgent today than in the United States and Canadian contexts in particular, and throughout Western nations in general.

AS GOES YOUR THEOLOGY, YOUR MISSIOLOGY, YOUR METHODS

Church planters must be outstanding theologians and outstanding missionaries. To have one without the other is a liability to the Kingdom. If our theological foundation is wrong, our missiology and methods are on tenuous grounds when it comes to the advancement of the Kingdom among a population segment or people group.

THE PENDULUM IN THE WEST

What is a church planter? In the United States, how is the church planter typically defined: as a missionary or as a pastor? In other words, in what direction does the church planting pendulum point (toward pastor or missionary) when it comes to a general understanding of the church planter in the twenty-first century in Western contexts? How do most of the books, conferences, blogs, and church planters themselves, describe the church planter—as missionary or as pastor?

For the most part, the Church in Western contexts operates from what I refer to as a pastoral missiology, rather than an apostolic missiology. The former typically develops in contexts where there is a mature Church that has existed over a lengthy period of time. A pastoral missiology understands and engages the mission field from a pastoral perspective, rather than an apostolic perspective. The pastoral perspective must be present in missional activity, but not to the exclusion or relegation of the apostolic perspective.

A DISCLAIMER

I want to note a few things at this point. First, I have many years of pastoral experience serving churches in the US. So, please understand, I am not attempting to pit pastors against missionaries.

Second, when I use the adjective apostolic, I am not referring to a denomination or a church. I am not referring to someone who is like the Twelve, who communicates extra-biblical revelation that is on par with the Scriptures. And I promise I'm not going off the deep end and getting ready to start preaching on late-night television.

I'm simply using a derivative of the New Testament Greek word that I believe communicates the New Testament truth regarding the nature of those whom churches send with the message of the gospel to plant churches. I think the word apostolic is better in this case than the Latin translation of *mitto*, from which we get the word missionary, with all of its historical and contemporary connotations.

Third, when missionaries function as pastors and pastors function as missionaries, frustrations and problems often arise in the Kingdom. Why? Simply because their giftings are distinct. One is not able to fulfill the role of the other. Problems come when people act outside of their spiritual calling. All the gifts of the Spirit are blessings to the Church, but their functions are separate and interdependent, and this is the way the Lord meant it to be.

Should missionaries be pastoral? Absolutely! Should pastors be apostolic? Absolutely! I think the Scriptures are clear on these matters.

But if our missionary methods come from our missiology that comes from our theology and advocates that pastors are should act as missionaries and missionaries should act as pastors, then we have a problem.

What I find surprising is that as long as we are applying the aforementioned statement to non-Western contexts, most evangelicals would agree with me. But attempt to make the application to a post-Christianized, Western context, and such is not the case.

APOSTOLIC MISSIOLOGY

Here is a quick summary of my description of an apostolic missiology. It is

- a view of mission that treats societies and peoples as a mission field should be treated—lost without Jesus and in need for the rapid dissemination of the gospel resulting in the multiplication of disciples, leaders, and churches.
- a view of mission that recognizes that the West has many local churches in existence—some ten, twenty, fifty, or one hundred or more years in age—and the structures and organizations took a long time to develop.
- a view of mission that seeks to sow the gospel seed into the hearts of the people, with the expectation that the Holy Spirit will birth His church in His time.
- a view of mission that allows for the development and application of simple, yet highly reproducible, methods that the new believers can be taught to use to preach the gospel and plant other churches.
- a view of mission that advocates that missionaries are never permanent fixtures connected to a new church, but rather exist as a scaffold for a season.
- a view of mission that desires to see contextualized churches, that are self-supporting, self-expressing, self-governing, self-identifying, self-teaching,

self-theologizing, and self-propagating churches planted from the moment the Holy Spirit gives birth to those churches.

- a view of mission that works hard to avoid falling into the trap of paternalism (i.e., new believers and new churches must depend on the church planters for everything because they can't "do church right") or the trap of pragmatism (i.e., that the goal is to get a church planted by any means that works to create the organization, rather than see the Kingdom expand).

- a view of mission that drives missionaries to reach, teach, empower, and release new churches to the power of the Lord and His Word (Acts 20:32), knowing that He is able to keep them from stumbling and to present them "blameless before the presence of his glory with great joy" (Jude 24).

- a view of mission that drives missionaries to follow the example of the apostle Paul who never abandoned new churches and made certain that the new churches were taught the whole council of God (Acts 20:27) and had their own elders (Acts 14:23; Titus 1:5).

Apostolic Missiology—Part 2

I wish to set before you a model of history to assist us in thinking about where most of us are in our view of mission that leads to our field practices when engaging Western societies. I am making broad generalizations to assist us in moving in a healthy direction for missionary labors.

As a society moves from an historical point in time when it was without the gospel to a time when its people became Kingdom citizens and developed a well-established Church, four shifts seem to occur:

FROM SIMPLICITY TO COMPLEXITY

When the gospel typically enters into a pioneer area, the message, methods, and models used tend to be simple in nature. While such is not always the case (e.g., use of the mission station paradigm), often the missionaries operate without much complexity. There is a desire to sow the gospel, teach the people simple obedience to the teachings of Jesus, and empower them to be the Church among kith and kin. Such biblical simplicity helps foster the rapid dissemination of the gospel and the multiplication of disciples, leaders, and churches.

Over time as the gospel continues to spread and the Church matures, infrastructures, organizations, and methods tend to become more and more complex. What began as missionary activity with few elements beyond biblical simplicity develops into a highly structured paradigm for ministry and mission.

Of course, such development is not always a bad thing. It is a sociological reality that most organizations move from the simple to the complex. Sometimes such structures and organizations are necessary for healthy growth and development. Problems arise, however, when such complexity hinders the rapid dissemination of the gospel and the sanctification of the churches.

FROM THE APOSTOLIC
TO THE PASTORAL

A developing leadership is needed for a maturing Church. Such is a good thing. What began as apostolic labors transitions to pastoral ministry.

As the number of Christ followers increases within a society, the need for such missional engagement diminishes. The need increases for pastor-teachers to oversee the new churches to equip them to do the work of the ministry (Ephesians 4:11-12). People are no longer asking the Philippian jailer's question (Acts 16:30), but rather "How do we now live as followers of Jesus?"

FROM APOSTOLIC MISSIOLOGY
TO PASTORAL MISSIOLOGY

As the Church becomes more pastoral in her function and less apostolic, missions in that society becomes filtered through a pastoral lens instead of an apostolic lens. This results in a pastoral missiology out of which the Church then develops on-going missionary methods. Evangelistic? Yes. But such is not sufficient if a sizable portion of the population requires missionary labors before they become Kingdom citizens.

FROM MISSIONARY METHODS TO PASTORAL METHODS

Remember, our methods are derived from our missiology. So, if a community of believers shifts from a view of mission being apostolic in nature to a view of mission being pastoral in nature, then the evangelism, church planting, and leadership development methods will reflect such shifts.

A result of a pastoral missiology applied to a post-Christianized context is generally a failure to think and function missionally, but instead to take a pastoral approach to missionary labors.

A pastoral missiology leans toward maintenance and the conservation of structures and organizations. Such is the nature of pastoral ministry—even for many of the most evangelistic pastoral ministries. And this nature is a good thing—for a pastor and an established local church. Pastors are called to be pastors. The heart of the pastor is rightly aligned in this direction for the sheep.

Unfortunately, a pastoral missiology misapplies this good desire to the mission field and finds satisfaction in the planting of churches with believers who have been

Kingdom Citizens for a long time, rather than with recent converts from the harvest fields. A pastoral missiology typically wants to maintain and control rather than empower and release others to be and function as the local church in their context. By way of an historical analogy, a pastoral missiology understands missionaries to be like a scaffold but desires that scaffold to remain attached to the building (i.e., the local body of believers), once the construction is complete.

As long as the society consists of a large percentage of believers, a pastoral model alone is many times sufficient for engaging the peoples; however, Western contexts have moved deeply into post-Christianized waters. Such a transition has now created the need for both pastoral paradigms and a return to apostolic missionary teams. If the Church operates with only one model, it is like trying to fly an airplane with only one wing. The Church in the West, particularly in the United States and Canada, has been attempting such an aeronautical impossibility for a long time.

Apostolic Missiology—Part 3

This is a difficult section to write, because I know how personal this material will be to many people. Remember, I'm right there with you. But while some of you may not be able to make such radical ministerial shifts at the moment, others can and will. And all of us can begin to teach healthy theology, which affects missiology, which affects missionary methods. I have no desire to discourage anyone, but to push us all toward good works.

What we have been doing in Western contexts, for the most part, is not healthy gospel-centered and gospel-driven church planting. And it is not sufficient to reach the four billion people who do not know Jesus.

BIBLICAL CHURCH PLANTING

The Scriptures do not tell us to plant churches. Rather, we are called to make disciples. So, biblically how are disciples made? By evangelism. Following conversions, we are to baptize and teach them to obey all that Jesus commanded. But it all begins with evangelism. Even when we move beyond the Matthean account of the Great Commission (Matthew 28:18-20) and into the book of Acts, we observe this model applied.

For example, on Paul's first missionary journey (Acts 13-14), he and Barnabas made disciples and then gathered them into new churches. Luke records what they did in the cities they had just evangelized:

When they had preached the gospel to that city and had made many disciples, they returned to Lystra and to Iconium and to Antioch, strengthening the souls of the disciples, encouraging them to continue in the faith, and saying that through many tribulations we must enter the kingdom of God. And when they had appointed elders for them in every church, with prayer and fasting they committed them to the Lord in whom they had believed. Then they passed through Pisidia and came to Pamphylia. And when they had spoken the word in Perga, they went down to Attalia, and from there they sailed to Antioch, where they had been commended to the grace of God for the work that they had fulfilled (Acts 14:21-26).

Did you catch it? Which came first, evangelism or the church?

When we examine Paul's first letter to the Thessalonian believers, we see the heart of a church planter in love with the people of God. In the first chapter, the apostle reminded them of how they became disciples, and what the Lord had been doing through their example:

For we know, brothers loved by God, that he has chosen you, because our gospel came to you not only in word, but also in power and in the Holy Spirit and with full conviction. You know what kind of men we proved to be among you for your sake. And you became imitators of us and of the Lord, for you received the word in much affliction, with the joy of the Holy Spirit, so that you became an example to all the believers in Macedonia and in Achaia. For not only has the word of the Lord sounded forth from you in Macedonia and Achaia, but your faith in God has gone forth everywhere, so that we need not say anything. For they themselves report concerning us the kind of reception we had among you, and how you turned to God from idols to serve the living and true God, and to wait for his Son from heaven, whom he raised from the dead, Jesus who delivers us from the wrath to come (1 Thessalonians 1:4-10).

Did you catch it? Which came first, evangelism or the church?

We cannot talk about biblical church planting until we can talk about evangelism. The biblical paradigm for church planting is evangelism that results in new churches.

THREE PRIMARY PURPOSES OF APOSTOLIC MISSIONARIES

The three primary purposes of biblical church planters are the following:

- Evangelism—reaching people from the harvest fields (Romans 15:20; 1 Corinthians 9:16)

- Discipleship—teaching the whole council of God, primarily done following the conversions (Acts 20:27; Ephesians 3:14-19)
- Leadership Development—raising up elders for the new churches (Acts 14:23; Titus 1:5)

I believe these three are self-explanatory, so I'll not elaborate.

POOR THEOLOGY

Remember, as goes your theology, so goes your missiology, and so go your methods.

It is not about planting churches. If our missiology is focused on planting churches, then as long as I am able to plant a church with a group of people who are already believers, I have accomplished the goal. I can start churches all day long—and have great worship music (which I love, especially if there is a heavily distorted guitar and/or a banjo involved), preach outstanding expository messages, and start amazing small groups—and if no one comes to faith in Jesus, then I have accomplished my goal.

More churches? Yes. More disciples? No.

It is not about planting churches. It is about making Kingdom Citizens who will live according to a Kingdom Ethic in covenant relationship to God and one another as the local expression of the Body of Christ. It is out of a disciple-making movement that church multiplication movements occur.

But this is not cool . . .

What happens if the receptivity level is low (and we're working faithfully to contextualize the gospel.)? What happens if my supporters are wondering why we have not started having a public worship service? What happens if my financial support is coming to an end and I have nothing to show for it—let alone a group of new believers who will support me financially as their pastor? What happens when my reports do not reveal the numbers that my partners desire to see? What happens when my fellow church planters begin to ask me how things are going? What happens when my vision does not come to pass and my strategy does not work out? What happens to my sense of self-worth when I don't have "results"? What happens when my results are not like those of that other church planter?

. . . we plant churches.

When evangelism gets tough and the fields are hard, we become weary and fatigue sets in. We forget about an apostolic missiology and begin to operate from more of a pastoral model.

Transfer-growth church planting begins to look very appealing to us and our supporters. In some cases, it is much faster in producing results and churches. For a long time we have been wanting to preach that great sermon series on the family, but all the unbelievers we have been evangelizing are still without Jesus. And there are many Christians out there who would definitely like to hear it and apply such biblical truths to their lives. For a long time we have been wanting to use the great youth curriculum that we have written, but still those unregenerate parents are still unregenerate and not interested in coming to our events. And there are many Christians out there who would definitely like to hear it and apply such biblical truths to their lives. For a long time we have been wanting to shepherd people according to the Scriptures, but those ungodly people will not repent and believe. And there are many Christians out there who would definitely love to be pastored by someone who would love them and teach them to obey all that Jesus commanded.

. . . and we begin to operate from a pastoral missiology. We begin to focus on planting a church with those who are already Kingdom Citizens.

. . . but we are not commanded to plant churches.

I think I just lost 87.3% of my readers.

❖ ❖ ❖

No Command for Church Planting

When I train others for church planting, one of the first things I tell them is that our work is not about church planting. Now, I recognize this is a strange statement for me to make, especially since I have written books and articles on the topic. Let me explain.

There is no command in the Bible to go into all the world and plant churches. The Church is never told to plant churches until the end of the age or search out all people groups and plant churches among them.

It seems everywhere we turn today, both churches and mission agencies in North America and outside this continent are training and sending missionaries to plant multiplying churches across the globe. Over the past twenty years in North America and Europe, numerous books and articles have been published addressing this topic. Conferences and practical resources are being provided every year to potential church planters. More and more seminaries are offering courses and emphases in church planting.

Then why is there so much talk about church planting if there is no scriptural mandate?

MISSIONARY ENDEAVOR

Our Lord is very clear about the Great Commission. The Church is to make disciples of all nations (people groups, not nation states). One of the best ways to fulfill this mandate of evangelizing, baptizing, and teaching obedience is through the planting of contextualized churches among the various people groups and population segments of the world. For it is in the process of evangelizing, baptizing, and teaching that local churches are planted. Church planting is a missionary endeavor. Our Lord gave the Great Commission before His ascension, and it was the Apostolic Church that later followed in obedience, setting the example of church planting for others to follow.

STARTING IN THE FIELDS,
NOT THE BARNS

Biblical church planting is evangelism that results in new churches. But churches can be planted with little to no evangelism being done.

For example, if our annual goal is to plant twelve churches, then all we need to do is gather some long-term Kingdom citizens together into twelve groups, lead them to covenant together as twelve local churches, and we have accomplished our goal. And if we do this, people will sing our praises and invite us to speak about church planting, telling them how they can plant twelve churches in a year. And no one will ask us about making disciples.

But it's not about church planting. We are called to make disciples—and the first step in making disciples is doing evangelism. For it is out of a disciple-making movement that churches are birthed (Acts 13-14). Unfortunately, most church planters in North America are more involved in gathering together long-term Kingdom citizens than doing evangelism that results in new churches.

AN EXERCISE

Let me give you a little exercise. The next time you hear about churches being planted, I want to encourage you to be radically biblical and simply ask, "How many people recently came into the Kingdom of God before these newly planted churches came into existence?" If you are talking with church planters in North America, do not be surprised to find out that the answer is generally few to none. Rather, than finding church planters who saw churches birthed out of the harvest field, you are more likely to find churches planted by the shuffling of the saints around in the Body of Christ.

Today, we plant the church first, and then (hopefully) lead the church to do evangelism.

If our goal is to plant a church, then our goal has been accomplished. Let's have a party and celebrate.

But it's not about planting churches.

THE COOLNESS FACTOR

But planting churches is cool! It is cool to quickly start a worship gathering with high quality music and preaching. It is cool to quickly develop church programs for kids, families, outreach, missions, etc. It is cool to be able to write to our partners in the ministry and show them "tangible" things that prove we have been at work—making good use of the resources they have sacrificed for our labors and hoping such partnerships will continue.

But it's not about planting churches.

Our mandate is about evangelism, baptisms, and teaching those new believers how to be the local church in their context. It is about teaching those new believers how to gather for worship. It is about teaching those new believers how to preach, how to pastor, how to lead children, families. It is about teaching those new believers how to do missions. There is not much that others can see, feel, and hear in the early days of a church recently birthed from the harvest. . .

. . . not much other than a group of new Kingdom citizens, agreeing to learn and live by this new Kingdom Ethic in covenant community. And this is messy, often-times a slow process, and gives us little to report to those back home. Definitely not cool.

Planting churches is cool; . . . making disciples out of the harvest that will become local churches is not.

But it's not about planting churches, is it?

❖ ❖ ❖

The Stewardship of Rockin' to an 8-Track in an iPod World

As a younger Gen Xer, I am old enough to remember the 8-track tape. With my formative years being in the 80s and early 90s, I later spent a small fortune on cassettes. Yes, I even had a few albums and 45s, but could never figure out why I would want to spend my money on something so bulky and easily scratched. I was slow to move into the world of CDs but quickly adapted when I saw their advantage over my well-worn cassettes and records.

The music remained the same—the mediums changed. The times changed. We all changed along the way. And, wow, we are thankful for such a shift!

Only the collector now invests in 8-tracks. A company would not continue to operate from a cassette culture in an iPod world.

Jesus said, "Heaven and earth will pass away, but my words will not pass away" (Mark 13:31). So true! But, we often take this statement to mean that the Christian cultures of the world will also remain as constants. We assume that while Jesus is the same yesterday, today, and forever (Hebrews 13:8), the Christian economies and the structures and organizations supported by those economies will remain till the end.

We assume that what was for our forefathers will be for us. So wrong!

It is an exercise in poor Kingdom stewardship when the Church constructs and becomes dependent on creations that should shift and even pass away. When our vitality is found in the temporal, we have missed the mark. Though we know this matter to be the case, we all still say together:

- I can't start making iPods, for my denomination only has 8-track players.
- I can't start selling iPods, for my income depends on the 45 record.

- I can't start developing iPods, for I have a B.A., M.Div., and Ph.D. in Cassette Tapes.
- I can't point others to iPods, for I will have no one left to listen to me.

Are we too dependent on blessings that were to exist for a season for gospel advancement? In the Kingdom, the music remains the same, but often the mediums are divinely designed to change.

If the iPod world is our reality, how should we live with warehouses full of 8-track tapes and new cassettes rolling off of the assembly line each week? Let's not take too long to figure it out—the four billion remain.

❖ ❖ ❖

Three Areas of Missional Adjustment in Our Flat World

We live in a flat world, one where the distant is near and the exotic is familiar. Unless present global infrastructures disintegrate, it is likely that the world will continue to shrink in the days to come. Technological, economic, and travel advancements will accelerate the pulling of the continents together into a virtual and practical Pangaea.

Widespread contextual shifts demand that the Church make wise adjustments to the missionary strategy in making disciples of all nations. While the truth of the never-changing gospel that was once for all delivered to the saints remains (Jude 3), wise stewardship involves methodological adjustment with the ever-changing contexts.

Our shrinking world is creating a great amount of pressure on the Church, particularly related to sending disciple makers to the nations. While such stress has numerous implications on Kingdom service, I briefly want to draw our attention to three significant practices that need to occur in our efforts related Kingdom expansion.

PRACTICING STRATEGIC INTEGRATION

Missionary strategies for "over here" must be developed in light of our missionary strategies for "over there." For centuries we have often thought of domestic missions and international missions as two strangers on two different paths that should never cross. While there remains significant distinctions between near-culture evangelism (i.e., E-0 and E-1) and distant-culture evangelism (i.e., E-2 and E-3), global shifts are forcing the Church to return to a much healthier biblical missiology and truly recognize the world as our parish, without continuing in an unhealthy dichotomy of home and foreign missions.

Better communication and planning needs to take place among Kingdom citizens scattered across the nations. Better communication and planning needs to take place among church leaders overseeing such local church missionary activity. Better communication and planning needs to take place among mission agencies.

We must move beyond the philosophy of this land is my land, this turf is ours, to the understanding that the world is our field.

DEVELOPING MAJORITY WORLD PARTNERSHIPS

If denominations and churches should be integrating their strategies for global disciple making, the next obvious matter is that such integration will require developing partnerships with local churches in other nations. While I recognize that such practice has been taking place among some Kingdom citizens and that there are numerous challenges to such partnerships, wise stewardship in this new day will seek to develop healthy relationships between churches in the West and those in Majority World nations.

For those of us in the West, we will feel the tension between paternalism and an abdication of our responsibility. We must not repeat the problems of the past; however, we must not discard the wisdom and experience the Father has provided for us. Just because colonialism was bad for missions does not mean that all Majority World churches are healthy. Yes, mistakes were made; however, past problems are not justification that the West should just step aside and let the Majority World carry out missionary labors (as some have been advocating). Do we have much to learn from our brothers and sisters? Yes! But do we have much to contribute as well? Yes!

LABORING AMONG THE DIASPORAS

There are 232 million people presently living outside of their countries of birth. Many of these peoples are followers of Jesus and many are not. We need to consider how best to minister to, through, and beyond the diasporas. Some are Kingdom servants in need of equipping and encouragement, a potential powerhouse for the multiplication of disciples, leaders, and churches. Others have traveled land, air, and sea and are in need of the good news for themselves and their people.

We live in an age of migration, a time of such mass movements unlike any other in history. It would be wise for us to reflect deeply on Acts 17:26-27 as we recognize the Kingdom opportunities now present among the peoples on the move. I wrote *Strangers Next Door* hoping to raise awareness among churches in the West of this present reality. The movement of the nations is one of the most critical issues shaping the Church in the twenty-first century. Unfortunately, many of us are not aware of the global realities and the Kingdom potential.

I recognize that change is not easy. And the longer we have been traveling one path when it comes to Kingdom labors, the more difficult it is to adjust to new directions. As stewards of the mystery of Christ, we must seek the

Father for wisdom to make course corrections, for patience with those who are not quick to see the opportunities before us, and for unity in the Body as the world watches.

It is easier to talk about these three adjustments than to do them. But we must start somewhere and talk can be valuable.

How about having that difficult conversation with someone today concerning these areas?

❖ ❖ ❖

20-Year Priority

Twenty-two years ago I told Jesus I was willing to pastor His people. Twenty-two years ago. Much has happened over this period of time. Much has changed; much has remained the same.

One matter that has remained for the past two decades is the priority of our disciple making and church planting efforts in the United States and Canada. We continue to give priority and attention to working among reached people groups. This is true among my denomination and most other denominations, networks, districts, associations, and churches in North America.

By the 1980s and 1990s, most evangelical denominations working outside of North America had embraced Winter's 1974 call to the "hidden peoples" of the world, with the highest priority being that of cross-cultural evangelism. We never embraced this focus in our own context.

We still have not embraced it—even with an estimated 540 unreached people groups living in North America.

Twenty years of giving priority to the reached at home, at least since my calling began.

Don't you think after twenty years it is time for a change?

How about an unreached priority for the future?

Can we try it for the next twenty years? Or, at least ten?

❖ ❖ ❖

That Deer-in-Headlights Look

"Where are the greatest needs in the United States for planting churches?" My immediate response usually is something like, "Go to the 300,000 Indian Hindus in New York. The 60,000 Somalis in Columbus. Or, consider the 60,000 Punjabi in New York. How about the 20,000 Yemeni just down the road from them? The 18,000 Pashto in San Jose? Serve among the 16,000 Kurds in Nashville. (All of these are unreached people groups, some with few or no known believers among them.)

And the general response I get? That deer-in-the-headlights look.

When it happens, I feel that a shock to the system has occurred and a moment is needed to recover, reorient, and reengage in the conversation on a different level.

And I often think, why?

Why is this a common reaction? Is it because

- this many internationals cannot be in the United States?
- unreached people groups are not in this country?
- church planting is not about planting churches from out of the harvest but beginning with long-term Kingdom citizens like us?
- anyone desiring to serve as a church planter in North America should not be a missionary?
- cross-cultural disciple making only takes place overseas?
- such needs don't exist here?
- there are few equipping and support systems in place for those doing such labors?
- such challenges are only to come at missions conferences, urging people to go to other countries?

And when I ponder why evangelicals often respond this way, I also find myself with that frustrated look of a deer in the headlights.

It is long past time for North American evangelicals to get out of the headlights, open our eyes to the realities around us, and change our language, missiologies, methods, strategies, structures and organizations when it comes to making disciples of all nations. What is it going to take in your circles of influence to see such change? What is it going to take in mine?

Let's lift up our eyes and look at the fields . . . and stop staring into the headlights.

Brace Yourself

You have a heart for reaching unreached peoples in the United States or Canada. Great!

Brace yourself.

Whenever you approach your pastor, network, association, district, mission agency, or peers, they will share in your excitement but are unlikely to know what to do with you.

If you had told them you wanted to reach the unreached in India, Indonesia, Iran, or Iraq, they would have known immediately where to point you for direction, resources, networking, coaching, and training. But, you told them you wanted to reach an unreached people group in Indiana (or Iqaluit, Canada).

They will rejoice with you.

They will pray for you.

And when you ask them for guidance, you will likely get the deer-in-the-headlights look.

We know mission . . . over there.

Do we really know mission . . . over here?

Maybe what we think we know we really do not know.

Reaching Yemen via Dearborn

I recently returned from Dearborn, Michigan, which is part of Metro Detroit. This community is home to the largest concentration of Arab Muslims in the United States, many of which are from Yemen, Lebanon, and Iraq. During our time there, we visited three mosques and spoke with several long-term residents in the area.

On one evening about 7:00 pm, we entered a particular mosque and were greeted by ten men and young boys. After introducing ourselves and asking a few general questions about the mosque, we were invited to sit on the floor to talk. Surrounding the four of us were people from Yemen, Egypt, and Bangladesh. For the next hour-and-a-half, we spent time in discussion with these men and boys about Islam and the gospel of Jesus Christ. We listened. We asked many questions. We learned. We preached Christ.

They took pictures with us.

We took pictures with them.

At 8:30 pm, everyone recognized that the boys needed to go home and go to bed. The next day was a school day. It was time to leave.

When we stood to leave, one of the men from Yemen (who had completed a pilgrimage to Mecca) approached us and through broken English inquired, "You come to my home for dinner?"

Later that evening, I could not help but think of how easy it was for the gospel to reach the ears of these men and boys, the majority being from Yemen.

The population of Yemen is 27 million. All of the 17 people groups making up the population of Yemen are considered unreached peoples. And within these 17 groups, 15 are listed as unengaged-unreached, meaning that no intentional church planting strategy is happening among them.

The threat level for missionaries serving in Yemen is listed as severe to chronic. The physical challenges for serving there are considered strenuous.

If you have read my writings, you know the greatest needs for disciple making and church planting are outside of North America. No doubt about this fact; however, let's think about this interaction in Dearborn for a moment.

It is an hour-and-a-half flight from Birmingham (my home) to Detroit. We simply walked into a community from Yemen, showed respect and love, and shared Jesus to a captive audience.

Threat level?

No one yelled at us.

No one threw us out of the mosque.

No one shot us nor stabbed us.

We were invited into a Yemeni home for dinner after an hour-and-a-half of interaction.

Physical level?

Well, I guess it was a little strenuous climbing over a three-foot brick wall and walking down an alley to get to this mosque. My feet did fall asleep because of the way I was sitting on the floor of the mosque. That was really uncomfortable, until I changed my sitting position.

When will we recognize that the migration of the nations is for the reaching of the nations (Acts 17:26-27)? What will be said to the Church in the United States on that Day? We had a reputation for traveling the world but were not willing to cross the street to reach the strangers next door?

❖ ❖ ❖

Unreached People Groups in the West

"God cannot lead you on the basis of facts you do not have," so noted Ralph Winter (*Mission Frontiers*, Jan-Feb 2007). While I do not completely agree with this statement—because God is not limited by our ignorance—there is a good deal of truth to be found here. God generally guides His people based on their understandings of reality.

Joseph knew a famine was coming so he led a nation to prepare for it.

Nehemiah was moved to build the wall based on a report of the physical and social situation of Jerusalem.

The Present Reality: We evangelicals have better data on people groups in some of the most remote places on the planet than we do in our own neighborhoods in North America. This is a crying shame.

Consider that most individuals and churches do not know

- that a very large number of unreached people groups (UPGs) live in the United States and Canada (I estimated 541 in *Strangers Next Door: Immigration, Migration, and Mission*);
- what groups are here and their populations;
- the percentage of believers—if any—among these unreached people groups;
- who is already ministering to some of these peoples.

However, among the other 6,000 unreached people groups across the world, we have a great deal of information including (but not limited to)

- where they live;
- percentage following Jesus;
- any known churches among them;
- any portions of the Bible available in their languages;
- population sizes;
- who are the groups ministering among them.

We should be upset. The main reason is that the Lord has brought many unreached people groups of the world to our communities, and we in the United States and Canada are not aware of this reality and the potential for gospel advancement across North America and the world. Such is a matter of stewardship, and we have failed greatly in this area.

The United States is the world's largest immigrant receiving nation. And both Canada and the United States are very ethnically diverse with the peoples of the world (Canada more so than the US). The United States is the third largest country in the world in population. Canada is geographically the second largest country in the world; therefore, researchers being able to provide quality data that is beneficial to missionary strategy face great challenges and a great deal of work. But it can be done.

The reality is that these two countries are two of the most researched nations on the planet. General academia has a great wealth of data already to assist us. Evangelicals easily have the people, churches, and the financial resources available to do what is needed.

While we rallied the troops to understand the unreached people groups in the 70s-90s, we failed to organize for such domestic labors. We not only are reaping the problems of such oversight in the United States and Canada but have limited our work overseas as well. For example, how many of the UPGs who are strangers next door to us, who if reached, would be the gateway into many of those peoples we've been trying to reach for decades in their home countries? Our myopic missiology treated missions as a one-way street, while teaching us that domestic mission was mainly evangelistic outreach.

The good news is that conversations are occurring that address this problem. Unfortunately, these conversations are several decades late—a much too common trend among evangelicals. But something is better than nothing at all. I hope.

God can lead us, even in our ignorance. But in His economy He sure seems to honor and lead in a more specific manner when His people are good stewards with their resources—which involves knowing their contexts. Remember what He did with men like William Carey and Ralph Winter—who did their research and shared it.

What are your thoughts on this topic? Does it surprise you that we know less about the peoples living among us than we do about them in their countries of birth?

❖ ❖ ❖

Kingdom Steward
Thought of the Day

This country is home to the third largest number of unreached people groups, behind India and China.

Most church planting in this country is among reached people groups.

This country is 26% evangelical and has about 360 unreached people groups.

What country? This country is the United States.

❖ ❖ ❖

Oaxaca to Bakersfield: Removing the Barrier between Foreign and Domestic

I want to draw your attention to Valley Baptist Church in Bakersfield, California. Here is a church that asked about the unreached "over there" and came to see them "over here" as well. You should read the full story by Emily Pearson, "Missionary Helps Church Find Its Embrace People Group," at stories.imb.org.

In 2011 Valley Baptist decided to reach the Tijaltepec Mixteco people of Mexico. At that time they were an unengaged-unreached people group, meaning that not only were they less than 2% evangelical but also no known church planting strategy was being implemented to reach them (There still remains approximately 3000 unengaged-unreached people groups globally.).

As the church began to reach into southern Mexico, they quickly learned that the Tijaltepec Mixteco were living in their backyard. Co-pastor Phil Neighbors commented, "To our amazement, we found out that 25 miles from us are approximately 700 of our people group. They had migrated from Oaxaca, Mexico, here to work in the Central Valley of California."

The church decided to reach out to this unreached people group for a fellowship event. About 400 Mixtecos showed up.

In addition to their church planting labors in Oaxaca, the church has started twelve Bible studies among the people in Bakersfield with plans to plant a church!

It is my prayer that more and more churches across the world would recognize the Kingdom potential of the movement of the nations and our responsibility as Kingdom stewards. We live in the age of migration and are witnessing the outworking of Acts 17:26-27 in an unprecedented way. The Divine Maestro continues to orchestrate the movements of the nations for His glory.

Now is the time to recognize the importance of an integrated mission strategy—melding together the foreign and the domestic—when it comes to reaching unreached people groups!

Until the strangers next door are strangers no more!

❖ ❖ ❖

A Double Standard for the Unreached

Since researchers Barrett and Johnson (*World Christian Trends*) told us years ago that only 0.1% of Christian monies collected goes toward the unevangelized world, evangelicals in the United States have rightly cried, "Inappropriate!"

Their stat preaches well.

This number makes for passionate blog posts.

It will rally the troops.

Yes, we need to reallocate our expenses and people and time, too.

Yet a double standard is at play. Some of the very ones advocating more for the unreached "over there" are the very ones doing very little to reach the unreached people groups living in their US and Canadian neighborhoods.

Are the greatest needs outside of North America? Absolutely! And more, much more, must be freed up for reaching the unreached in other countries.

If we are going to rail against the 0.1%, saying that more should go elsewhere, let's also make sure we are doing more to reach the unreached peoples here.

Consider these facts:

- The overwhelming majority of church planting efforts in the United States and Canada are taking place among reached people groups, not among the 540 unreached people groups living in North America.
- The overwhelming majority of our financial resources being spent in the United States and Canada is being used for ministry among reached people groups.
- The overwhelming majority of our "missionary" time is allocated to reached people groups.

It is time to drop the double standard.

❖ ❖ ❖

Over Here for Over There? A Future for Short-term Missions

Imagine the possibility of future short-term teams where the destination and unreached people group served over there is determined by the unreached people group your church serves over here.

> *Pastor, where in the world do you think the Lord is leading our church to go this year?*

> *Possibly Morocco. He has been at work among the Moroccans we have been serving in our community. Why should we attempt to create something new? Let's work where the Lord has already been working?*

Imagine the possibility of future short-term teams where the social connections of family and friends of unreached peoples over here are the bridges across which your church's teams travel to enter countries over there.

> *What are you doing in our country? Why are you here? I need to know before you are permitted to enter.*

> *We are staying with the relatives of Siaeem for the next ten days. He is a friend of ours from Texas.*

Imagine the possibility of future short-term teams where your church does not depend on missionaries over there to provide lodging or travel, and you only accept hospitality over there from the relatives of those to whom you minister over here.

Imagine the possibility of future short-term teams where your teams are received as insiders over there as a result of your church serving and loving unreached peoples over here.

Ja-lin has told us to hear what you have to say about God. She speaks so highly about you and has experienced your love and hospitality in Atlanta. Thank you for welcoming her into your community.

Can you imagine the possibility of what the Lord can do among the nations as we serve the strangers next door? The future of missions—particularly short-term efforts— begins to look differently when we recognize the importance of transnational social networks and the hand of the Divine Maestro orchestrating the movement of the unreached peoples into our communities.

Imagine the possibility of connections made at a well over here opening opportunities to serve in a village over there.

Many Samaritans from that town believed in him because of the woman's testimony, "He told me all that I ever did." So when the Samaritans came to him, they asked him to stay with them, and he stayed there two days. And many more believed because of his word. They said to the woman, "It is no longer because of what you said that we believe, for we have heard for ourselves, and we know that this is indeed the Savior of the world" (John 4:40-42).

We live in a highly integrated world. The world knows this. If only the Church would grasp this. Kingdom stewards are quick to recognize the hand of God among the nations in their communities and ask, "Can faithful service among the strangers next door over here lead to global possibilities over there?"

Is "Over Here for Over There" a future for short-term missions? It has already become a present reality for some churches. What about yours?

❖ ❖ ❖

Rethinking Short-Term Missions

Short-term missions is long overdue for an overhaul.

Projects abound. Many of us run throughout the world doing great ministry in many needy parts of the world, but little mission takes place.

Some of us have made great strategic progress in the area of short-term missions, recognizing the value of long-term partnerships instead a "this year here and next year there" approach. Let's keep up the good work with such partnerships that assist in facilitating disciple making and church planting.

However, such strides are not enough; a leap is needed. We need to rethink short-term missions in light of the movement of the nations across the world.

One of our church members recently was invited to Saudi Arabia. This came as a result of friendships with some Saudis that only began three months ago. He has spent much time with them drinking coffee and tea, playing sports, and sharing the gospel. They know where he stands; they know he desires for them to know Jesus.

Another of our members was recently invited to a Hindu wedding in India. This came as a result of friendships with some South Asian Indians in the city. This couple has spent much time with this Hindu man drinking coffee and tea, eating together in their home, and sharing the gospel. He knows where this couple stands; he knows that they desire for him to follow Jesus.

It is difficult to get into several places in the world where the unreached and unengaged reside. And, if we finally get in, we then have to find a way to connect with the peoples there.

But, when the peoples of the world invite you into their world, everything changes. You are no longer an outsider.

What if our churches entered areas of the world for a week or two at the invitation of the people themselves?

What if the people introduce us to their social networks?

Of course, all of this is dependent on reaching out to the strangers next door and connecting with them. For many of us, this is where short-term missions should begin.

Blurring the domestic and the foreign until the strangers next door are strangers no more!

❖ ❖ ❖

Most Critical Issue in Church Planting

Reality #1

Hello. I'm J. D., and I'm a pastor in your community.
Really? Where is your church?
Oh? Um. Our church has not started yet...

Reality #2

Hello. I'm J. D., and this is my family. We're with a new church in town.
Really? Where is your church?
Oh? Um. Our church has not started yet, but we will soon...
I thought you said you were with a new church.

Reality #3

Hey J. D.! I loved your web site, announcing the new church in our city, and your Grand Opening!

Yeah! I'm excited. The church is going to start on February 29!

And what will you be selling at your Grand Opening? The new Target store just had a Grand Opening last week.

<u>Biblical Reality</u>

In the New Testament

- we don't read about wandering pastors without a flock to shepherd.
- we don't read about apostolic teams announcing they are with a new church.
- we don't read about anyone declaring a local church's existence before it is birthed from the harvest fields.

The most critical issue facing North American church planters is an ecclesiological identity crisis.

What is the local church? Where does it come from?

Who is a church planter? Who is a pastor? What do they do?

The way to overcome the identity crisis is to return to the Book that provides our definitions. But, be warned. Once you start down that path, culturally preferred definitions, tribal expectations, personal comforts, and organizational infrastructure will push back with a great force.

❖ ❖ ❖

The Church and Adjectives

I ain't no good at English. I'm doin' much better now that I have been writin' fur some time. Maybe it was because I grew up in Appalachia. Maybe it was because I took advanced English in high school simply because the courses dealt more with literature and less with English. I think I was a doctoral student before I knew the difference between an adverb and an adjective.

So, who I am to write about adjectives? Well, I did read about them once.

In this section, I want to address a very common matter, particularly among the churches in North America. We are people who like our adjectives when it comes to describing the church. We have Baptist churches, Methodist churches, and Pentecostal churches when it comes to our denominations. We even have nondenominational churches to describe who is not officially connected to a denomination.

Now before I continue on with you assuming that I am opposed to adjectives, I must add that such is not completely the case. Personally, I am very proud to be a fourth generation Baptist of the Southern tribe.

Historically, we added adjectives to the Church to define where a particular church stood theologically. I am thankful that we make a distinction between Catholic and Protestant and Nazarene and Presbyterian. While I am not pleased with the acrimony and fall-out that occurred many times throughout history resulting in the multitude of theological adjectives we now have, I am thankful that many of us today are advancing the gospel together instead of warring against each other.

Of course, such theological adjectives are an historical development and a long way from simply the adjectives of "Jewish" church or "Gentile" church.

But now we do have adjectives such as "Russian," "South Asian Indian," and "Nepali" that clearly delineate the ethnic and language characteristics of these churches. Again, I'm thankful for this. If I accidentally walked into the meeting of a Chinese church on Sunday morning expecting to hear my language, I would be in for a surprise. My Chinese is not very good. I can't even correctly pronounce "General Tso's Chicken" in English!

But where will the adjectives end? Now, while I'm comfortable with theological and linguistic adjectives, I become more concerned with a new type of adjectival category that is now commonplace.

In North America today we have moved beyond classic distinctions of Protestant and Catholic, denominational, and linguistic differences to what I'll describe as distinctions in structure and flavor. While some of these may communicate significant theological distinctions, most do not. For example, on a regular basis, we now use the following adjectives to describe the local church: house, organic, simple, cell, multisite, mega, traditional, contemporary, conventional, postmodern, liturgical, emergent, multihousing, cowboy, biker, seeker, seeker-sensitive, hip-hop, college, multiethnic, and the list goes on and on.

As a missiologist I understand the benefit of such adjectives. I use them all the time. If we know what the ideal cell church looks like, we can better understand what someone communicates when they say, "I am a member of a cell church." My first book was titled *Missional House Churches*. While there are limitations, clearly the use of "house" in the title communicated something specific about the churches in the book.

I share this information to say that I recognize the value of the structural and flavor adjectives.

But my concern lies in three areas.

First, at what point does the use of adjectives become an activity in absurdity? Will there come a day when we speak of "Baptist, post-modern, seeker-sensitive, Gen-X, cowboy, house churches"? How's that for your business card?

At what point do our adjectives hinder the dissemination of the gospel and the growth of our church? By directly teaching the church who we are and who we are attempting to reach, we are indirectly teaching who we are probably not going to reach. Do we teach our Japanese churches that they are responsible for reaching African-Americans? Do we teach our cowboy churches that they are to evangelize and plant churches among the hip-hop subcultures?

Finally, regardless of the adjective used, we must always be faithful to the biblical prescription for all that is necessary for a church to be a healthy church. Whether the church meets under a banyan tree or in a multimillion-dollar facility is not the point. The timbre of the music is tertiary in nature. The denominational or nondenominational stance takes a back seat to what Jesus requires of His Church. The structure, ethnic composition, and whether or not the members ride Harley's or horses are irrelevant here.

While contextualization factors matter, missionaries must know the biblical necessities for a local church to exist. They must know the biblical characteristics of healthy churches so that they can instill within the DNA of those newly planted churches a vision and teaching for what our Lord expects.

Our biblical ecclesiology must come from the Scriptures and not from our missiology.

In a day when many individuals and groups have gone soft on the doctrine of ecclesiology, we must make sure we remain faithful to the biblical parameters. The good news is that Jesus knows best for His Church. He has told church planters what is expected. The borders He has established for healthy churches are wide enough to allow for much flexibility and diversity.

So, while we continue to have adjectives here, remember there is coming a day when He will wipe away every tear . . . and every adjective.

❖ ❖ ❖

When Talking about Church Planting Feels like Witnessing to Mormons

When I share the gospel with Mormons, one of the first things I do is establish our definitions. Without cutting to the chase and recognizing our definitional differences, it is difficult to then evaluate what we each believe in light of the Bible (the KJV, of course!).

Discussing church planting in most North American circles reminds me of witnessing to Mormons. Same words but different definitions.

The next time you start to say the words church planting stop and think: What am I talking about and what are they hearing?

The next time someone near you says, "church multiplication," ask yourself this question: What do they mean?

In North America we have definitional differences when it comes to church planting.

If you believe it is about gathering long-term Christians together to covenant as a local church, then say so.

If you believe it is about making disciples from the harvest and leading them to covenant as a local church, then say so.

If you believe it is about gathering a crowd for a worship gathering, then say so.

If you believe that church planting is something else, then say so.

One thing we should all know for certain is that the Bible does not tell us to plant churches. Our mission is not about church planting. (Hence, the reason I began *Discovering Church Planting* with the statement, "It is not about church planting.")

Once we have come to understand what we are saying, let's examine the Scriptures to see if what we mean needs adjustment.

When our vocabularies become saturated with words everyone uses, we begin to assume that we all know what we mean when we use such words. In the beginning when such words are unfamiliar and scarce, we generally have to state the word and our definition to establish common ground. Overtime we get tired of providing definitions. After all, we reason, everyone by now knows what we mean. Not true.

We used to do this with the word gospel. But then a bunch of wise stewards came along and rightly asked the question, "What do you mean?" Then they followed up with a biblical evaluation to determine if those commonly-held definitions squared with the Scriptures. If you want to know what happened after such inquiries were made, search Amazon to see how many "gospel" books have been published recently.

Church planting has become a ubiquitous expression and church multiplication is quickly growing in popularity.

We need to ask one another, "What do you mean?" and then move to biblical evaluation.

Definitions express our theology.

Our theology shapes our strategies and methods on the field.

Let's stop saying church planting, unless we can say what we mean. And after we say what we mean, let's evaluate one another to see if what we mean is in alignment with the Scriptures. This is extremely important when we have not been commanded to plant churches.

What if we check our definitions with the Scriptures and determine that what we have been saying for years (and developing strategies to support) is not what we should be saying and advocating?

I think you know the answer to that question.

Let's keep definitional differences to witnessing to Mormons and not in church planting discussions.

❖ ❖ ❖

What is Church Planting to You?

Is it about any of the following ideas?

- coolness
- being hip
- small groups
- glorifying God
- rental property

- making disciples
- starting a worship gathering
- keeping the 4 billion in mind
- marketing, mailers, and music
- beginning in the harvest fields
- reaching the unreached peoples
- developing the best website in town
- looking at the field and seeing one church
- acting on those thoughts about the 4 billion
- beginning with long-term Kingdom citizens
- having preview services and grand openings
- organizing the church before the church exists
- raising leaders from the harvest for the harvest
- raising enough money to start a small company
- bringing our desired cultural traditions to others
- being able to say, "Imitate me as I imitate Christ"
- teaching them to obey all that Christ commanded
- designing a killer kids' ministry for the community
- using strategies built with a philosophy of multiplication
- keeping things simple for the health of the new believers
- being a wise steward with your actions toward the 4 billion
- adding another flavor to the Baskin-Robbins of Christianity
- developing that church's website long before the church exists

- teaching obedience that they may be able to teach obedience to others
- seeing multiple disciples, leaders, and churches while looking across the fields
- starting one and hoping to do it again within three years—when we can afford it
- keeping things so complex and complicated that only a few could ever reproduce our methods

Church planting. What is it to you? Make sure you know before you go.

❖ ❖ ❖

Time to Enlarge the Church Planting Table

For too long we have been guilty of making church planting a ministry for only the high capacity, high caliber leaders. These are the individuals that I describe as the 8-, 9-, 10-caliber leaders. Now, while I am all for equipping and mobilizing such church planters, the reality is that such leaders are a minority in the Body of Christ. They are greatly needed for Kingdom advancement—but still a minority.

The examples prized in church planting today, particularly in the North American context, are generally reproducible only by this minority. The ecclesiology and missiology, while mostly not lacking biblical support, is often encased with a great deal of Western cultural expectations.

We have created a table for the 8-10-caliber leaders, with little room for anyone else.

It is time to enlarge the church planting table to make room for the majority of potential missionaries who are just as biblically qualified and called, but unable to support strategies, methodologies, and ecclesiologies developed by high-caliber church leaders.

What is most unfortunate is that while we would never turn away potential church planters who fall into the 1-7-caliber range, we ask them to come to the little table that is in place and pull up a chair.

We tell David to kill Goliath and expect him to wear Saul's armor. When he insists that he needs to remove such encumbrances, we permit it but look at him as if he has lost his mind. Maybe we have lost our minds.

It is time to enlarge your church planting table, making room for the majority of potential missionaries in the Body of Christ.

Pastors, you need to stop looking elsewhere for the high-caliber church planters you don't have to send from your churches and start equipping and mobilizing the 1-3's and the 4-7's that the Lord has entrusted to your care. Be faithful with what you have. If you have the 8-10-caliber leaders, then be faithful with them as well.

It is my concern that if we do not enlarge our church planting tables, then the church planting momentum that we are currently seeing in North America may soon come to an end. Any time we elevate, promote, and expect only that which can be reproduced by the few, we show just how unwise we are when it comes to being a good steward with the Body of Christ. Just look to the 1970s for the smaller churches that could not "do" Sunday school or have bus ministries like the few churches that were set forth as the model to achieve. Consider the 1980s and 90s for the church growth methodologies that only the few were able to reproduce. We created the atmosphere that "If you are not doing it their way, then you are not doing well." One consequence of these once widespread trends is that when the majority realized that they were not able to reproduce the models, frustration and apathy set in.

I do not want to see church planting become something that was trendy, and "now it is time to return to what we can do for Kingdom advancement." I do not want churches to look at the present trends and say, "Well, if that is church planting, then we do not have what it takes."

The way to help churches realize that they have what it takes is to change the definitions, expectations, the measuring rod.

So, how big is your church planting table in your denomination, network, or local church? What are you pointing others toward as the way to do it right? Have you created expectations that will set up the majority for failure?

As a leader, if you are only reading the books and attending the conferences geared toward the minority of potential church planters in North America, you need to change directions.

It is time to enlarge our church planting tables, making room for the majority. If we do, we are likely to be much closer to experiencing the multiplication of disciples, leaders, and churches that we all desire.

There are over 4 billion people in this world without Jesus. About 75% of the population of the United States and 80% of the population of Canada also falls into this massive number of lostness.

I think we need everyone we can get to the table. Don't you?

It is time to put some extra leaves in our tables and add a lot more chairs.

❖ ❖ ❖

Plant the Church that is, Not the Church to Come

Hasty expectations hinder the birth and multiplication of churches.

Plant your churches, just make sure they have all of this stuff, and these structures, and these activities, and these twenty-five marks, and these forty-one purposes, and this affiliation, and give that amount of money.

Such is okay when we start instant churches with long-term Kingdom citizens.

They have years of sanctification. They have a long history of church cultural expectations. We should expect much from such churches, for much has been given to them.

But planting instant churches is to be the exception to our strategies, right? There is a place for it; however, we should permit it as the exception, not the expectation. It is not a regulative paradigm in the New Testament.

Such theology is important, for it keeps us from having unrealistic expectations for churches planted with new believers. These churches just started the sanctification process.

Don't expect them to manifest a maturation level as a church that is ten, twenty, or fifty years old.

Don't strap them with things our Father expects for them to grow into overtime.

Don't hinder the babes by telling them they must be running immediately; they just started crawling.

Are they a regenerate, baptized group who self-identify as a local expression of the Body of Christ? Have they covenanted before the Lord and one another to live out the Kingdom Ethic (found in the Word) in relation to God, each other, and the world—not fully understanding what all that means, but because Jesus expects it they are willing do it?

If so, then you have planted a church that is poised for the multiplication of disciples, leaders, and other churches. You have planted the church that is.

For now, teach them the Word and how to study and apply the Word in private and in community. The Spirit and the Word will sanctify them. All of those marks, purposes, manifestations, and expectations will come as they are built up in Christ (Colossians 2:6-7; 1 Peter 2:1-5).

That is the church to come.

❖ ❖ ❖

Jesus Did Not Say to Wait for Pastors to Plant Churches

The United States is not only one of the world's largest countries, it also home to the third largest number of unreached people groups (a story few have heard). Over the past several years, I have noticed a very common church planting strategy that is on the minds of most churches, agencies, and networks:

Wait for the Lord on high to send a pastor to you—one from among that unreached group, be he French, Chinese, or Indian—to reach those people with the gospel and plant a church among them.

Granted, near-culture evangelistic work is often more effective than cross-cultural work (but not always); however, the problem with this thinking is that we run into a problem if we want to reach the unreached, among whom few believers and no pastors exist.

When was the last time you had a conversation with a Somali pastor? Saudi pastor? Wolof pastor? Or, what about a pastor representing the other 540 unreached people groups living in the United States and Canada?

The Lord only told the early believers to wait in Jerusalem for the coming of His Spirit (Acts 1). Even when He told them to pray for laborers for the harvest, it was in the context of them going to make disciples (Luke 10:2). He has told us to go, to cross the cultural gaps, to make disciples of all nations.

He has not told us to wait.

He has not told us to look for pastors to go and plant churches among those people.

But where will the pastors for those people come from?

From the same location where He has provided all of the pastors in the world today—out of the harvest.

Cross-cultures in your neighborhood. Do evangelism. Make disciples from the harvest. Baptize them. Gather those new believers together in a small group. Teach them to obey. Lead them to covenant together as a local church. Raise up pastors from among them to shepherd that new congregation (see Acts 13-14).

Jesus said to go and make disciples, not wait for pastors to plant churches.

❖ ❖ ❖

Your Church Is Closer to Planting Than You Probably Think

One of the reasons why most churches do not participate in church planting is that they believe it to be something grandiose and outside of their reach. Pastors often listen to the exceptional, ten-talented, high-capacity church planter and assume that one must be like him to do church planting the right way.

> *We don't have a guy like that in our congregation; we can't plant a church. Our church is made up of managers, teachers, bankers, electricians, welders, servers, stay-at-home moms, college students, mechanics, accountants, physicians, painters, and contractors.*

We hear of complex church planting methods and elaborate systems and assume that such is necessary for a church to be planted. We look at our people and think the task is just too great for our congregation.

We often cast a church planting vision before our people and leave them there. While the vision may be good and right, it often requires the execution of complex methods that only the rare ten-talented guy can manipulate. Church planting involves a series of small steps that are not beyond the grasp of churches.

Since we are talking about planting a church and not starting worship services, gathering a crowd, organizing kids programs, renting property, buying buildings, preaching a sermon series through the book of Leviticus, developing a website, creating a mass mailer to be distributed to 10,000 people, raising enough money to start a small company. . . . (you know, all of those potentially good things that come with established churches comprised of long-term Kingdom citizens), let's begin with the basics.

Your people can see themselves involved with the basics. You can see your people involved in the basics. After all, the fundamentals are simple. They are basic. They are absolutely necessary.

RECOGNIZE THE BASICS

Church planting is very difficult work. It is a ministry that is on the edge of Kingdom expansion. It involves intensive spiritual warfare. We only need to look at the missionary labors of Paul to understand that the spiritual oppositions are great. Church planting is hard. Very hard.

However...

Church planting is not complex. In fact, it is very simple (see 1 Thessalonians 1:1-10 for the requirements). It is a task for both the educated and uneducated, the literate and illiterate, and the full-time employee and the unemployed.

Church planting is evangelism that results in new churches. The beginning point for the church planting team is not with long-term Christians. The team begins with unbelievers. The movement begins with sharing the gospel and does not move to a gathered group of Christians until new disciples have been made.

The new believers are then taught obedience in community with one another (i.e., small group). Finally, the small group is taught from the Bible what the church is and does. The new small group is then challenged with the question, "Is the Spirit leading you to unite as a local expression of the Body of Christ?" And, if so, such begins a wonderful journey of the team with the new church to raise up and equip elders who will then equip the church for the work of the ministry.

QUESTIONS TO ASK

If you are trying to lead your people to be involved in church planting (or maybe you still have not caught a vision for it yourself), then ask your people a few questions:

1) Can you and two or three people from our church share the gospel with other people? Can the three of you set a twelve-month goal—by the grace of

the Lord—that you will work to see nine people (for example) come to follow Jesus (three new believers per team member)?

2) Can the three of you gather those new disciples into a small group in which you will begin to teach them how to follow Jesus? Can each of you mentor these nine outside of the weekly group time (three new disciples per team member)?

3) Can you and your team model the Christian lifestyle before this new small group while leading them through an intentional study of God's word regarding what is the local church?

4) After studying through the Word about what is a local church and modeling individual and body life, can you and your team ask the small group if the Spirit is leading them to be a church?

5) If they decide to self-identify as a local church, then can you and your team begin working with them to raise up elders whom you and your team will begin to spend more time developing as leaders for this body?

SMALL STEPS

Pastors, are your mechanics, teachers, stay-at-home moms, managers, and college students sharing the gospel? Are your plumbers, servers, and business owners teaching one another the Word and having fellowship in small groups (Sunday school, home fellowships, family groups, etc.)? If so, then your church is much closer to church planting than you probably think.

Whenever we remove much of the hype, quantitative expectations, and North American cultural expressions of church planting, we come to recognize that church planting is not very glamorous. It involves small steps. It is about making disciples from out of the harvest and teaching them to obey all that Jesus commanded. If your people can do this, then by God's grace, your church can plant churches. Many churches.

But, if we cannot make disciples, gather them, and teach them to obey, we have a problem—a problem much deeper than believing that our church cannot be involved in church planting due to the lack of money, high-caliber leaders, excellent musicians, and so on.

❖ ❖ ❖

When Missionaries Want to Drink Sweet Tea from a Garbage Can

I was once in Auburn, Alabama, teaching a seminary class. Part of this missions course was taught online and part in the classroom. I traveled to the city to spend a week with the students. It was a blessing to be with these guys.

I am a lover of Bar-B-Q and sweet tea. Of course, when these guys came to realize this outstanding element of my character, they suggested that we have lunch at Mike and Ed's. I had no hesitation going to this fine eatery.

Upon arriving, I was surprised to find the sweet tea being served from a very large garbage can. Only in the South.

Yes. We did drink sweet tea from the garbage can. I did not understand it. It was unusual. But it was good!

What a crazy act. What a crazy concept. No one drinks from a garbage can on purpose and likes it so much that he or she is willing to pay to do it.

Yet, Mike and Ed's is making a killing off of it.

AN AXIOM ALL PASTORS SHOULD KNOW

Missions is messy, and you need to be mentally prepared for what is to come once you start down this path.

MISSIONS AXIOM: *Missionaries do strange things.*

These Kingdom servants never say, "We've never done it that way before." To them everything is new. They are entering into the fields. They are starting with nothing and moving toward something. They do not begin with structures and organizations; they begin by entering into the kingdom of darkness to bring out the captives into the Kingdom of light.

Typical, normative, routine, predictability—these words are hard to find in their vocabularies.

Instead, we generally find them most familiar with terms such as *uncertainty, pioneering, chaos,* and *instability.*

THE EXPERTS ARE IN THE FIELDS

Missions does not happen in front of a computer. Church planters are in the trenches. They are missionaries living and functioning in the highways and hedges of lostness.

As a result of them being in the heat of the battle, they are the experts when it comes to their contexts.

Now for many of us, traditional approaches to evangelism and ministry have worked very well. The Lord used that 1975 Baptist Hymnal and "Victory in Jesus" to bring us to faith and sanctify us. You remember how He worked for years through your church's bus and van ministry to reach all of those kids from the nearby community. And what about those great block parties we used to have. It was so wonderful to see what the Spirit did to advance the gospel.

Maybe such methods will still be effective with the unbelievers your missionaries are laboring among. But maybe not. I don't know their contexts. And my guess is that you do not truly know their contexts either.

BE LEARNERS, BUT HOLD THEM ACCOUNTABLE

So, let's ask them to educate us. Let's ask them to tell us about the people groups and population segments among whom they are serving. Let's ask them to tell us what is working and not working to reach the people with the gospel, gather them, teach them, and raise up leaders among them.

But when we ask them such questions, we may need to fasten our seatbelts and be ready for a surprise. They may tell us about methods they are using that we have never considered. They may share approaches that we would never dare to implement in our established church ministries. They may tell us tales that make us uncomfortable.

But if our missionaries are remaining true to the Scriptures, being good stewards with their resources, and not participating in unethical or illegal practices, let's give them the freedom they need to serve on the frontlines of Kingdom advancement.

We must absolutely hold them accountable but not be absolute with our methodological convictions. They know the context better than we do. They are living and breathing it every day. Let's trust them. We should ask the tough and challenging questions. We should push back where necessary and provide correction where necessary.

It is not about giving them free reign but rather the freedom to fulfill their ministry.

Pastors, don't be surprised when your church planters one day share with you that they are planning on drinking sweet tea from a garbage can. Push back on them. Be discerning. Ask challenging questions. Hold them accountable. Speak wisdom into their lives. And, if at the end of the conversation, you believe their approaches are appropriate, then pray for them and encourage them in their labors.

If we do, we may find that very soon we are filling our cups with them and discovering some great Bar-B-Q in the process.

❖ ❖ ❖

Church Planters – What Do You See?

My family and I recently watched "A Christmas Carol." You know the story. Scrooge is visited by different spirits trying to provide him with different perspectives on his past, present, and future. Each apparition challenges him to see his world from a different angle.

At times, we all need a change of perspective for God's glory.

As I was reflecting on the numbers of church planters with whom I have worked, taught, and equipped over the years, I could not help thinking about the need for most church planters to see things from a different perspective. Consider the following perspectives of this question:

What do you see when you observe a field of 100 people who do not know the goodness and grace of Jesus?

Most church planters see a future with some of these people declaring God's glory.

But why only some? What about a future of all of them declaring God's glory?

Most church planters see a future church.

But why only one local church? What about 4, 5, 7, and maybe even 10 churches in that field of 100 people? Do you see the churches yet to be birthed by the Holy Spirit and then to spend years growing in sanctification?

Most church planters see a future church with them serving as the pastors.

But why are you the pastor? What if in that field of lostness there are several pastors yet to oversee those new churches? Do you see men coming to faith and being recognized by those churches as their pastors? Do you see these pastors in need of your missionary ministry to equip and release them to be the shepherds the Spirit has called them to be? Can you see yourself shepherding the shepherds?

Most church planters see a future church that is involved in planting other churches, usually 2, 3, or 4 years or more after the first church is birthed.

But why so long? Can you see the immediate multiplication of disciples, churches, and pastors that results in the rapid dissemination of the gospel across social networks, spanning the 4 billion people on earth that also do not know the goodness and grace of Jesus?

Why is such a change in perspective so important? Because it challenges us to return to the Scriptures for the theological foundations on which our missiology and church planting methods are to be constructed. Such a change requires us to ask the Lord of the Harvest what He has to say about a field of lostness, church planting, and the raising up and training of pastors. A shift in perspective leads us to ask if we are being good stewards of the mysteries of the gospel that have been entrusted to our care, for our time, according to the Word of God. We are confronted with the question, "Are we doing good things for the Kingdom at the sacrifice of doing the best things for the Kingdom?"

Scrooge had to have a shock to his system before he changed his perspective. Let's change ours now before Marley shows up.

Now. . .

What do you see when you observe a field of 100 people who do not know the goodness and grace of Jesus?

❖ ❖ ❖

Take Courage, You are not the First Domino

We often fail to consider the work of our Father before we arrive on the scene.

We wrongly think we are the first domino to fall in God's plan when it comes to our missionary endeavors. We may be near the beginning, but we are not the starting point, even among the unengaged and unreached. He is the starting point.

We move into town and forget about His general revelation (Psalm 19:1-4; Romans 1:19-20).

We begin our work on October 4th, but He has been at work before the foundation of the world (Ephesians 1:4).

We grab a table in the coffee shop, prayerfully considering how we can reach those around us, and we have no idea that an angel of God is appearing to Cornelius down the street (Acts 10:3).

We develop important strategies to reach the nations, but often fail to remember that He has determined where and when the nations will live so that they would feel their way toward Him (Acts 17:26-27).

He is at work before we arrive. Do we realize and rest in this important truth?

And while He is always at work, He has chosen to work through His Church to proclaim the gospel so that everyone who calls upon the name of the Lord shall be saved (Romans 10:13). Yes, He has a means as well.

He is a missionary God. He is more concerned about the salvation of the nations than we are. He is more invested in the birth of churches than we are. He has a missionary strategy. His strategy involves us. We are colaborers with Him (2 Corinthians 6:1). And that is good news!

Take courage in your labors today. You are not alone.

And even while we sleep and face the multiple, mundane, daily tasks of life, His dominoes are already falling in place.

❖ ❖ ❖

No More Muddin' and Pullin' for Jesus

While the concepts of mudding and truck and tractor pulling are prevalent throughout the United States and Canada, there's a part of me that wants to say that those recreational activities developed near my hometown. Growing up in Corbin, Kentucky, I had a few childhood moments when I was honored to participate in these up-and-coming Olympic sporting events. Whether it was in a Jeep, seeing what my Honda XR80 could do in the woods after a massive rainstorm, or attending the local truck and tractor pull, playing in the mud was fun.

(For those of you not familiar with the haute culture of muddin' and truck/tractor pulls, I'll let you Google them.)

I remember attending a tractor pull and standing on the sideline. The massive machine would be hooked up to a specially designed wagon containing an enormous amount of weight. The driver would rev his engine to an ear-splitting-decibel level. As the engine would roar, sometimes fire and smoke would belch forth from the exhaust. When the signal was given, the tractor would attempt to plow down the muddy field, pulling the load to the finish line. Generally, the front end of the tractor would rise off the ground as the enormous rear tires would spin like crazy, attempting with all of their tenacious might to gain some traction in the inches of mud. Rocks would fly and mud would be thrown for yards. The driver with the best time was declared the winner.

As I reflect on these times in the mud, I wonder if many times our approaches to missional engagement with the peoples in our contexts are similar to the spinning of wheels that occurs at such outdoor events.

Take a tractor pull for example. An enormous amount of energy is used to move the vehicle forward. Part of the required energy is related to the massive weight that the tractor is pulling. But it is the mud and lack of traction that contribute to the major energy drain. And it is the mud and spinning (and sometimes going nowhere) that makes the event worthy of our participation.

I am concerned that we get so caught up in doing tasks and being busy for Jesus that we rarely move forward in the multiplication of disciples, leaders, and churches. We make a great deal of noise. There is much excitement, but we creep along. And whenever we do accomplish our goals, we expend such an enormous amount of our resources (time, money, people) that we are too exhausted to carry on. Of course, we celebrate the few small victories. But we really get excited over just doing activities, regardless of the outcomes.

If ministry was a sprint, we would be doing great. But ministry is a marathon.

But what if instead of a few small victories on the way to accomplishing our Kingdom goals, our Father wanted us to experience several major victories? Such would be wonderful and welcomed, but a lack of wisdom and stewardship would keep us from them.

While there are times when faithfulness and calling require that we spin our tires for a season, we have to use discernment and ask, "Why are we always spinning our tires, slinging mud and rocks, and never moving forward?"

This question is a dangerous one to ask, but must always be asked by Kingdom citizens. The danger, of course, lies in the fact that such a question generally results in us being faced with a decision to make change.

And change is never easy.

The asking of this question is likely to bring some discomfort and possibly pain. We may discover sin in our hearts. It may reveal that our theology, missiology, strategy, institutions, structures, and/or methods need (radical?) adjustment. This question may reveal that we have substituted cherished traditions for wise stewardship. We may discover that we love our politics and popularity more than we love the King. Such a question may reveal that continuing in the status quo will not bring about what the Lord desires to accomplish through us.

The lack of progress that comes from a failure to make necessary adjustments for gospel advancement is not to be celebrated.

We have limited resources, but we have everything we need to do what our Father has called us to do. Let's not waste them.

Let's have enough courage to serve the Lord with faithfulness while it is still day. Let's not allow the substitution of the good for the best. Let's give it our all, and if we find ourselves spinning our tires for too long, let's make the necessary changes and move on. There is no room for muddin' and pullin' for Jesus in the Kingdom. Too much is wasted as a waiting world wastes away.

So, where do you see the slinging of mud and the spinning of tires? How are you going to respond as a Kingdom citizen?

❖ ❖ ❖

Taking the Shortcut in Missions

Every morning I take my children to school. And every morning we enter into the crazy car pool drop-off line. Crazy? Yes! Efficient? Well, that depends on whether or not you are in a hurry.

All the parents enter campus and snake their way around the school's property until they reach the designated drop-off point. This traffic pattern requires that one drive across eleven speed bumps, while moving very slowly. Now, while this trip circumscribes most of the school's property, the cars continue to move. There is very little stop-and-go traffic.

It's a slow process but efficient and effective for moving hundreds of cars in a short period of time . . . while not running over the kids.

Could this process be faster—maybe allowing me to save some time and have that time to grab an espresso or latte? Absolutely! But what would it cost?

Any recalcitrant parent needing their Starbucks fix could easily take the well-known shortcut, cutting their lengthy cruise across campus down to a matter of seconds. They could easily miss most of the speed bumps, hitting only two. They could be on and off the school's property in a very, very short period of time.

But . . .

This disruption of the normal flow of traffic would cause a great delay that would ripple throughout the hundreds of cars already in the car pool line. This interference would cause a breakdown in the entire system, hijacking effectiveness (and efficiency) for everyone.

As I dropped off my kids this morning, I could not help thinking about the great temptations that exist to shortcut the Church's call to make disciples of all nations. Sometimes the shortest and seemingly most efficient route to accomplish the goal is *not* the healthiest way.

Sure, it will win the sprint for us. But after the sprint is over, we may be very surprised to realize that the race is actually a marathon. And we just ran out of energy!

What about you? Are there missiologies, ecclesiologies, philosophies, strategies, and methods presently being applied in your country that appear to be efficient but not effective for the task to which the Church is called? Are there any shortcuts being taken that look very efficient and successful but are likely to result in poor health and chaos later?

Sometimes the drive around the building is the best way to go. Sometimes it is right and good to miss the opportunity to get a cup of coffee.

❖ ❖ ❖

Complex King, Simple Ways

Others have said this statement, and there is some truth in it:

> *In Jerusalem, mission was about movement. In America, mission is about business and enterprise.*

I want to make a slight adjustment:

> *In Jerusalem, mission was about simplicity (to know nothing but Christ; to preach Christ crucified). In America, mission is about complexity.*

And complexity often hinders church health and multi-plication.

The complexity of the Kingdom is found in the King not in His commands.

"But the word is very near you. It is in your mouth and in your heart, so that you can do it" (Deuteronomy 30:14).

Complexity is found in the One who spoke and the universe was created. Complexity is found in the mystery of the incarnation. Complexity is found in the substitution-ary atoning sacrifice for our sins on the cross. Complexity is found in the resurrection from the dead. Complexity is found in our conversions. Complexity is found in both Jew and Gentile being baptized by the Holy Spirit. Complexity is found in the new heaven and the new earth.

Complexity is not found in the apostolic work of the Church to do evangelism that results in new churches comprised of new Kingdom citizens.

When the gospel arrives in a new context, it generally comes with simple preaching and the demonstration of the Spirit's power (1 Corinthians 2:1-5; 1 Thessalonians 1:5). Over time churches that were once very simple in their expressions become very complex in their organizations. While complexity is not necessarily a bad thing, it can eas-ily cause generations who are born (and born again) into such complexity to think that such is necessary for healthy church life, ministry, and multiplication.

Church planting in many areas of the world's post-Christianized contexts will require churches to return to an apostolic simplicity. Such is presently the case in the United States.

Part of our present challenge is that the Church exists in a state of complexity. Most of our churches can do little without countless hours of meetings and discussions. Whenever we decide to do something related to Kingdom advancement, we then have to print up T-shirts for everyone to wear before we can do it.

Complexity.

We believe we can do little without large sums of money, years of extensive training, and leaders who if not connected to the Church would easily be able to create Fortune 500 companies or become the next Prime Ministers of small countries.

Complexity.

The present state of the world is that there are over four billion people on the planet who have no relationship with Jesus, and over two billion of those have never heard the name of Jesus. If our Lord's last words to the Church were to make disciples of all nations, should not the Church be willing to make radical adjustments to matters that stand in the way of getting the gospel to these peoples and planting churches among them so that they may obey all that Jesus commanded?

In light of His simple command, we should be asking ourselves how complex are we making the planting of churches as the fields remain white for the harvest?

We may be laboring hard but are we laboring wisely?

Missional stewardship drives us to ask such questions.

We are just scratching the surface of what needs to be done in the West. And we have been scratching for a long time. We have defined missions as something too complex for too long.

What needs to be done is something simple, biblically simple.

Call me idealistic, but our complex King has some very simple ways. Now, if I can just find that mustard seed.

❖ ❖ ❖

Tweaking the Structures for Movement

Some people are anti-structure. They think it is cool to be against "the man," but all for movement.

However, there is no movement without structures. Structures are necessary for health and multiplication. It was true in the first century; it is true today.

But not all structures will do. Some hinder the dissemination of the gospel and the multiplication of disciples, churches, and leaders.

Some people work for movement, but only if it will happen within their parameters–even if those structures fall into the hindrance category.

And when the desired outcome does not occur, they tweak.

And tweak.

And tweak.

The tweaking of structures–a revision here, some change there–might not result in sufficient posture in preparation for a movement of the Sovereign Spirit.

If 5, 10, 15 years of tweaking have not been sufficient, wise Kingdom citizens stop tweaking and start asking:

> *Do our structures hinder the multiplication of disciples, churches, and leaders?*

If the answer is yes, more tweaking is generally not the appropriate response.

How long have you been tweaking? Is it time to start asking?

Innovation

Status Quo and 2 Billion to Go

Status quo: the existing state of affairs.

Innovation: the act or process of introducing something new.

When it comes to healthy growth and multiplication, leaders must keep these two definitions in mind. While it seems cool to say, "I'm against the status quo; I'm all for innovation," such is not the way of Kingdom citizens. The existing state of affairs is not always evil. While there are times such matters deserve a wrecking ball, generally, this is not the case. It is often not helpful for Kingdom advancement when we destroy what has been developed over years, decades, and sometimes centuries.

Also, we should refrain from saying, "I'm against innovation; I'm all for the existing state of affairs." This is unhealthy as well. Kingdom citizens must be engaged in innovation. The world is a place of constant change. We must be students of God's world and respond appropriately. The failure to innovate is an example of poor Kingdom stewardship.

The book of Acts is filled with examples of the Church innovating while building on that which was already established. The widows were not neglected because the gospel needed to advance into new areas (Acts 6:1-6). The Jerusalem Church was not dismantled because the half-breed Samaritans received the Holy Spirit (Acts 8). What was established in Jerusalem and Samaria did not unravel when the Spirit baptized the Gentiles (Acts 10:44-48; 11:19-30). The Jerusalem Council did not require a discarding of matters in the Gentile world (Acts 15:1-35). Paul and Silas did not give up and go back to Antioch when their strategy was interrupted (Acts 16:6-10). Throughout the book of Acts, we read of a Spirit-led Body of Christ on mission in a world filled with pressures and change. While the existing state of affairs was not being scrapped for something new, there was a continual need for adjustment in light of sanctification, unreached peoples, and gospel proclamation.

Innovating upon the status quo is a good thing—being locked into the existing state of affairs is bad.

In light of the two billion people in the world who have never heard of Jesus, we must not lock ourselves down with the status quo.

In light of the two billion people in the world who have never heard of Jesus, we must build upon that which has gone before us.

❖ ❖ ❖

Stewardship of Innovation

The Church has always been called to a stewardship of innovation. While this terminology has not existed across 2000 years, the expectation has always been present. We may rarely speak using such language (something I hope changes in our time), but the biblical model for innovation is ever before us.

Innovation of this type is not the equivalent of that which occurs with a technology company or fast food corporation. The Church is not in the business of secret discoveries and shipping new products to market before someone else. Rather, the stewardship of innovation involves following the Spirit into a world filled with multiple pressures, as we carry out the Great Commission and make necessary changes.

And there is the issue of change.

Most local churches, denominations, agencies, and institutions do not like change and are not structured for change. We evangelicals are the utmost conservatives when it comes to our organization and structure. We are often slow to change; and once we do, we set such organization and structure in concrete. While stability is necessary for mission, such actions may reveal just how resistant we are to any future change and the Spirit who leads us to change.

If . . .

Jesus is building His Church, then we should expect change (Matthew 16:13-19).

Remember, He is intimately involved with His Church (Matthew 16:18, 19; Acts 9:4).

If . . .

we are filled with a dynamic Spirit, then we should expect change (Acts 1:8).

Remember, He is intimately involved with His Church (Acts 1:5; Ephesians 5:18).

Therefore . . .

the stewardship of innovation means we must anticipate and make wise adjustments as we labor for the multiplication of disciples, leaders, and churches. Sometimes such adjustments are small; sometimes such adjustments are massive.

The call to follow Jesus is a call to remove from our vocabularies the phrase, "We've never done it that way before." Innovation often takes us in new directions while building on the labors of those who have gone before. A reading of Acts makes this very clear.

Throughout the book of Acts, the Church often had to innovate for mission as the Spirit led into new frontiers. As Kingdom citizens, we are often required to change our general ways of thinking and functioning for the health of the Church and gospel advancement. Structures, institutions, organizations, and traditions are to remain nimble and held loosely. When the Church resists Spirit-led change and the need to innovate in light of global circumstances, we soon find ourselves impotent in a world of need.

Expect change.
Embrace the old.
Engage the new.

❖ ❖ ❖

Innovation in Mission

My family and I recently visited Epcot in Orlando. It had been several years since my previous visit. We had a great time on the rides and visiting the World Showcase area in the park. One particular attraction caught my imagination.

Spaceship Earth—the ride that is found within the golf-ball-looking structure at the park's entrance—was a fascinating 16-minute journey through time, showing innovations in technology that resulted in significant global changes. Beginning with the development of papyrus and culminating in the cyber age, the observer is exposed to a quick glimpse at how innovation leads to major breakthroughs that result in significant outcomes.

GLOBAL ISSUES

My book *Pressure Points* addresses twelve major global issues (including growth of cities, poverty, Diasporas, and what is truth) that are presently shaping the face of the Church. With each of these issues the Church is faced with a decision: follow the leadership of the Spirit and in-novate methodologically and strategically or remain on the present course.

The choice to follow the latter option is a recipe that will result in the hindrance of gospel advancement and church multiplication across North America and through-out the world.

In our globally integrated world, the issues in our own communities are found in communities "over there" as well. Issues do not limit themselves to geographical borders. Any denomination, parachurch organization, network, or local church that embraces a missiology limited and defined by geopolitical boundaries will find it very difficult to navigate the currents of change neces-sary for effective mission work in the world today and tomorrow.

INNOVATION IN THE BIBLE

But before we come to believe that innovation in mis-sions is rocket science, we must remember that such is not the case. In the book of Acts, we read that innova-tion to overcome significant barriers to gospel advance-ment was a matter of following the leadership of the Spirit of mission. For example, see Acts 10 (the reception of the gospel and Spirit by the God-fearers in Cornelius' house), Acts 11 (the birth of the Church in Antioch), and Acts 16 (the birth of the Church in Philippi). In each situation, the believers were required to change their general way of functioning and thinking; however, once the institutional/organizational adjustments were made—sometimes with great reservation and sometimes by force—the gospel continued to expand beyond the sociocultural barriers.

Jesus will build His Church (Matthew 16:18). This is not a matter for debate. The question of concern should be: "Will He work through us to build His Church?" We need to understand the challenges of our times, be filled with the Spirit of mission (Ephesians 5:18), and adjust our methods, strategies, organizations, and institutions accordingly. It is a terrible mistake to avoid Spirit-led innovation.

THE PAIN OF THE CHALLENGE

Unfortunately, such adjustments are usually painful and difficult. And, it is sad to write, that in many cases, until our pet preferences become a burden to us—or are cataclysmically removed from our control—we are likely to hold on to them, grieving the Spirit while believing we are walking the straight and narrow path for gospel advancement.

The Body must always be growing in conformity to the Head. And innovation is required with such growth. We do not innovate for the sake of innovation. We innovate for the advancement of the gospel as the pressures of age apply force and create challenges to the mission of the Church.

And just as the history of mankind is filled with examples of innovation that resulted in breakthroughs that reshaped society, the Church's innovations in missions will continue to result in breakthroughs that will glorify the Lord and reshape the Bride as She waits for the Groom.

What are your thoughts? Do you see any value in innovation in missions? Are there dangers with innovation? If so, how can we avoid that which is unhealthy?

❖ ❖ ❖

More of What We Know

Question: What do we do when we don't know what to do?

Answer: We do more of what we have been doing.

This is not the way of wise Kingdom stewards.

To do more of what we know is safe. It is comfortable. It fits with our longstanding systems, organizations, strategies, and traditions.

But we have a decline in baptisms, membership issues, money problems, fewer people going to mission agencies, seminary enrollment challenges, and lostness continues and the unengaged-unreached remain.

We do more and more of what we know, expecting change, hoping the challenges will be overcome, and expecting new results.

We believe what we have done to get us where we are will be sufficient to carry us to new vistas. We forget that to get where we are today required previous generations to make systemic shifts in their methodologies.

The hard decisions of that generation created our comfort zones for today.

More of what we know is not sufficient for the next level. Creating a new veneer is not sufficient. Rearranging the deck chairs will buy a little time, but we've already tried most of the possible chair formations.

Such is not the way of wise Kingdom stewards.

More of what we know is only sufficient for a season. And that season has passed.

❖ ❖ ❖

Two Steps Few Leaders Take

We're no longer going to believe that if God wants the heathen saved, He'll do it without us. We're going to use means.

We're no longer going to work only along the coastlines; we're moving to the interiors of these countries.

We're no longer going to build mission stations; we're going to focus on indigenous (and later, contextualized) *church planting.*

We're no longer going to think of the nations as geopolitical states; we're going to recognize that they are ethnolinguistic groups—unreached peoples (and even unengaged).

It takes a wise, bold, Kingdom Ethic-guided, Spirit-filled leader to question the present reality and ask if there is a more excellent way allowed by the Word. This is wise stewardship. This is a major step toward Kingdom innovation. Few leaders take the step to think differently about their realities. Culture, tradition, and systems are powerful forces. To think differently is unthinkable.

A second major step involves not just thinking about the unthinkable but actually acting upon such thoughts. Even fewer leaders are willing to walk this path. Too much is at stake; stability is often king; however, those that do are the ones convinced that He "is able to do far more abundantly than all that we ask or think" (Ephesians 3:20).

Few leaders take these steps. But, five to ten years after they do, we're often thankful they did.

Five to ten years from now (Lord willing), will others be thankful you took the two steps that few leaders take?

❖ ❖ ❖

Too Busy to Think

One of the disciplines that I have attempted to develop over the years is that of thinking. No, I am not referring to the dilemma that I experience when trying to decide what to get at the Krispy Kreme counter. But thinking on a much greater level. A macrolevel-type of thinking.

All great leaders are thinkers. They spend a significant amount of time in thought with the Lord regarding the tasks He has set before them for the day, week, month, year, and next several years.

But some misguided folk advocate that thinking is a waste of time.

"You are not paid to think. You are paid to crank out your daily quota of widgets on the assembly-line of life to which you are called."

But let's stop and consider this logic for a moment when it comes to the Kingdom. Unfortunately, such individuals do not realize that they cannot afford to keep you from using your God-given wisdom.

Whenever we stop and take significant time to think about what we are doing, we enter into a Kingdom activity that displays wise stewardship. Done correctly, such thinking adds strategic value to what we are doing for the Kingdom. When we stop and think

- we may discover that there is a more efficient way to crank out those daily widgets;
- we may discover that there is a way to crank out more widgets;
- we may discover that there is a way to improve the widgets;

- we may discover that there is something out there that is better for the Kingdom than cranking out the daily widgets (Oh, yes. I forgot to add that thinking is a dangerous thing.).

I find that I am not the leader that I should be when I am not intentionally setting aside time to think about my ministry and share my thoughts with our Father. A few hours set aside each week for reflecting on the previous week and the week to come is a very good practice. Also, try to schedule one and sometimes two days every month to spend with the Lord, thinking about what He has called you to do and where He is leading you in the future.

(Just as a side note—I have found that I have to spend more and more time with the Lord as He increases my responsibilities.)

For the sake of the Kingdom, start thinking. Each week or at least once per month get alone with God and His Word. Go old school—take a notebook and ink pen. No computer or iPad—too many temptations to distract your thoughts.

I usually come away from these times refreshed and challenged. My fellowship is strengthened and prayer life deepened. Sometimes I even come away with the sense that the Lord is preparing me for something else, but is not ready to reveal the details.

When we are too busy to think, we are too busy.
And that's something to think about.

❖ ❖ ❖

Change the Atmosphere;
Change the Culture

It is difficult to create a culture of multiplication. In order for most denominations, networks, and churches in the West to create a culture of multiplication, they need to experience an atmospheric shift.

What is an atmospheric shift? It is a change in the ethos of the group. It is a change in the things that are prized, rewarded, expected, encouraged, and emphasized.

We must remember that as goes our theology, so goes our missiology, and so goes our church planting methods in the field. So, yes, your church, district, network, and denominational leaders need to be not only outstanding missiologists but also outstanding theologians. One without the other is detrimental to the task at hand.

So, lets work it in reverse. Our missionary methods applied to the field come from our missiology. Our missiology comes from our theology. Recognizing that no multiplication of disciples, leaders, and churches happens apart from the sovereign work of the Spirit, let's ask ourselves some questions based on working in reverse:

- If we desire multiplication, will our present evange-listic, discipleship, and church planting methods get us there? If not, why not? Is something wrong with our missiology (e.g., understanding of missions)?
- If there is something problematic with our under-standing of missions, is this related to our theol-ogy? If so, what area or areas? Is it a Christological issue? An ecclesiological issue? Some other issue? Remember, being theologically conservative and biblically correct are not always the same thing.

As a leader in your district, denomination, network, and/ or church, I would ask you to consider prayerfully thinking through these issues.

If leaders do not take responsibility and lead—especially when it comes to changing the culture—it is not likely to hap-pen. If the change does not take place in your heart, mind, speech, and actions, then is it not likely to occur among those you lead.

Change the atmosphere; change the culture.

What are your thoughts on these matters? Do you think an atmospheric shift is needed to begin the cultur-al shift? Do you think problems are related to theologi-cal, missiological, and/or methodological issues? Maybe I am not asking the right questions? If not, what questions should we be asking?

❖ ❖ ❖

How Well Do You Know Your Missiological Box?

Dan Pallotta has written a helpful post for the *Harvard Business Review* titled, "Stop Thinking Outside the Box." In this work, he challenges his readers to understand the present box in which they find themselves in order to innovate and move beyond their limitations to health and growth. Consider his words:

> *You cannot possibly think outside the box unless you understand the nature of the box that bounds your current thinking. You must come to know that nature deeply. You must have real insight into it. You must accept it, and embrace it at some level, before it will ever release you.*

Pallotta's exhortation is helpful to us. How well do we understand our present circumstances on a biblical and missiological level?

Some of us understand our circumstances very well. Some of us have a very poor understanding of our circumstances. Kingdom stewardship involves ongoing evaluation of our present realities. We must resist the gravitational pull away from such reflection and take time to pray and think.

A desire to move beyond the box is often noble but not sufficient. Accurate understanding is critical. For "desire without knowledge is not good, and whoever makes haste with his feet misses his way" (Proverbs 19:2).

Innovation in ministry is not done for the sake of competition or simply to be cool. The Church does not innovate just to be innovative. We innovate for the advancement of the gospel as the pressures of age apply force and create challenges to the mission of the Church.

Spirit-led innovation involves us knowing our present theological, missiological, philosophical, organizational, and structural realities.

The truth is that Jesus will build His Church (Matthew 16:18). But will He work through us to do it?

We must understand the box in which we presently find ourselves in order to make the necessary shifts for gospel advancement and church multiplication. Of course, this reality will differ from denomination to denomination, country to country, church to church, and individual to individual.

❖ ❖ ❖

More Right Turns

UPS truck drivers rarely make left turns. Such turns are more dangerous to make than right turns. They also save the company money. By making 90% of turns to the right, UPS has been able to save 10 million gallons of gas (Matt McFarland, "The Case for Almost Never Turning Left while Driving," *The Washington Post*, April 9, 2014).

Drivers traveling greater distances to avoid idling time and going against the traffic flow have reduced emissions, increased delivery time, improved safety performance, and helped their bottom line.

Who would have thought? Only after the company began tackling vehicle performance did they see their limitations and come up with this right-turn model.

I can't help wondering if many of us in church leadership are busy, busy, busy for the Lord and rarely evaluating what we are doing and how well we are doing it. Maybe even making a great deal of left turns, idling in traffic, and going against the flow—thinking that such a flurry of activity is the way in the Kingdom. Much activity is definitely life on the assembly line—a true American value. But, we're not trying to crank out a quota of Kingdom widgets each day. Right?

Doing a great deal of activities may get us kudos, but it may not be the best action for Kingdom stewards.

Ponder the path of life, for the foolish fail to do so (Proverbs 5:6). Evaluate. Such is the way of the Kingdom steward. Once we do, we may realize the need to minimize—or even eliminate—left turns.

❖ ❖ ❖

Right Questions Matter

There are many questions to be asked about church health and mission. Many are being asked with the right heart. But right motives are no guarantee that the right questions are being asked.

We often ask questions with familiarity in mind. This is a good place to begin, but we can't remain here. Unfortunately, we often stay put. We have not learned the stewardship of questioning.

The right questions matter.

If you were in the recording business and someone started asking you questions about manufacturing 8-track players, you would quickly know the wrong questions were being asked.

Similar situations are found within the Church when it comes to some discussions regarding health and mission.

When we fail to discern the wrong questions, we fail to ask the right ones.

The right questions matter.

The 4 billion remain.

❖ ❖ ❖

To the World through the Stomach

For sometime I have wondered about the potential of using the culinary passions and skills of Kingdom Citizens to reach into parts of the world where few are able to go.

Why? Because I believe the way to the heart of many people is through their stomachs. No, I am not referring to feeding the poor—though that could most definitely be included in my thinking. Rather, I am pondering the potential of using the gastronomic interests of the peoples of the world to open doors for ministry opportunities.

The reality is that people like to eat. And we are presently in a period when many of the peoples of the world want to share their cultures with those not of their cultures. Cooking is a way to connect with people.

Imagine if the cooks in the Kingdom were to take their regional cuisines on the road to share with other peoples of the world, while sharing in the foods of others. What opportunities would arise through these connections?

My hometown of Corbin, Kentucky, is the home of the first Kentucky Fried Chicken restaurant. The Colonel started frying it three miles from my backyard. And if this Southern-influenced fast food chain can now be found across the world, why can't regional cooking open doors for sharing the good news with others? (Okay, you health food junkies, no snide posts about any "ethical" issues related to both sharing the gospel with others and Southern US cooking that hardens the arteries and facilitates heart disease.)

Maybe those annual church recipe books can tie into a greater missional purpose.

What are your thoughts?

❖ ❖ ❖

Share Today's Stories Later Today

We hear stories from the corporate world about research and development departments spending large sums of money to keep everything a secret until the product is ready for release. Corporate spies, insider information, classified documents, and top-secret information are constantly matters of concern.

Such is not the way of life in the Kingdom. We are not trying to roll out a better cell phone before our competitor down the street. We understand this to be the case; however, sometimes our practices betray our beliefs.

We fear telling today's stories because we don't have all of the bugs worked out yet. We don't want to share what we are doing with others until we've got it right. We go underground with an idea and practice, sometimes for years, before tweaking it to perfection and then launching it to the masses.

Again, we are not trying to figure out the perfect hamburger before opening shop and talking to investors.

We fear sharing stories that make us look like we don't have it all worked out. Of course, we'll tell our success stories and leave out most of the things we did wrong. We fail to see the value in transparency and revealing what is not working very well. Remember, the conference you need to attend is the one no one is willing to host.

By the time we figure out what is working, take to the speaking circuit, and publish a book, we are years beyond that particular move of the Spirit. While the Lord is not limited, He works within social contexts. This means that by the time your church hears my success story, culture has shifted. Contexts are ever changing. Society moves on. And your church is now five to ten years late to the game.

We must learn to compress time for the sake of the gospel. In our highly integrated and globalized world, it is poor stewardship to fail to share what is working and not working in the moment.

I serve as the pastor of church multiplication with The Church at Brook Hills in Birmingham, Alabama. My primary responsibility involves equipping our members to multiply disciples and churches from the harvest fields. I often receive calls from leaders in other churches wanting to come to Birmingham to talk about what we are doing in the areas of leadership development, church planting, and pastoral training. My response always involves saying that I will share everything we are doing, that all matters are not resolved to my full satisfaction, and that I have more questions than answers at times.

One of the reasons I welcome these conversations is to give away what has been entrusted to us, even if we are only two years into the journey. I want other churches to take what we are trying to do (warts and all) and improve upon it for the advancement of the gospel among the nations.

No top secret R&D department.

No hiding, no concealing, no embarrassments.

No "what will they think if we share this now only to see it tank later."

No sharing only what is working well and avoiding discussion of what is not.

Sharing today's stories later today is the way of the Kingdom steward.

❖ ❖ ❖

Evangelical Ethos of Parachurch Entitlement – Part 1

I have always been supportive of parachurch organizations.

I was heavily involved in a Christian organization while a student at the University of Kentucky.

I earned two degrees from a seminary.

I served with a mission agency for nine years.

I taught as a Bible college professor at three different schools and as a seminary professor for fourteen years.

I am currently an adjunct professor for a seminary.

I speak several times each year to parachurch leaders and members of their organizations.

Every church I've pastored has financially supported the parachurch agencies and institutions of my denomination.

Our church partners with several different parachurch organizations.

Much of my ministry has been and continues to be connected to parachurch ministries.

I have always been supportive of parachurch organizations.

However, my concern is that many parachurch organizations have not worked toward the completion of the parachurch purpose but have created an evangelical ethos of parachurch entitlement. Rather than empowering local churches, many have become an end unto themselves.

Ask most parachurch leaders if God's plan is about the church or the parachurch and they will immediately say, "The Church, of course!"

The Church is Plan A. There is no Plan B. We know that.

Everything needed to make disciples of all nations is found within the Church. Everything needed for the sanctification of the saints is found within the Church. God did not birth the Church and the Parachurch.

Such Kingdom innovations are not necessarily bad things if done within the context of Kingdom parameters.

But if parachurch groups establish definitions of successful ministry that local churches are unable to achieve, we have a problem. The problem becomes compounded if local churches agree to such definitions. When the latter happens, we find ourselves in an atmosphere of parachurch entitlement.

Evangelical Ethos of Parachurch Entitlement – Part 2

As a fourth generation Baptist of the Southern Tribe, I'm all about cooperation—cooperation with those of my tribe and cooperation with like-minded evangelicals (a.k.a., Great Commission Christians) of other tribes. Such cooperation is with other churches and with parachurch organizations. It is biblical. It provides synergy. The wise Kingdom steward recognizes that making disciples of all nations is too much for one church to accomplish.

However, among some North American evangelicals, cooperation has inadvertently resulted in cases of code-pendency. Some parachurch organizations that originally were established to foster cooperation for Kingdom advancement, overtime have fostered a welfare mentality among churches.

Many local churches have the belief that they can't move unless the parachurch tells them they can move.

We can't go to the field because the agency did not approve us.

We can't go to the field because the agency did not have the money to send us.

I wonder what the early Moravians would think about this.

We can't call him as our pastor. He doesn't have a seminary degree.

I wonder what the Methodist and Baptist churches on the American frontier would think about this.

We can't reach the 3000 unengaged-unreached because we don't have any partners near them.

*We can't reach that people; they don't have the Bible
in their language.*

We often can't because of the definitions we subscribe to.
He, who holds the definitions, writes the story and con-
trols the movement.

Again, if any agency or institution creates a definition
of effective ministry that is outside of the present or future
grasp of the local church, such a definition is unbiblical,
even if the Church agrees to it. If the local church is by-
passed, the plan is unwise.

To agree to the definition is to agree to the story.

To agree to a story that is not about cooperation, but
codependency, is not a good thing.

Some of the greatest Kingdom advancements have
come through the work of parachurch ministries. For these
and those organizations laboring with the local church in
mind, I am grateful and look forward to what is to come.

However, no ministry should be done to keep the local
church from its biblical responsibilities—even if it agrees
to abdicate those responsibilities to the parachurch.

An option for wise parachurch organizations is to
work themselves out of their present jobs and into new
ones. Such is good missiology. They should not be designed to perpetuate their present existence until Jesus
returns.

They should be designed to empower, partner with, edify, and exhort the local church to biblical tasks. They should not be islands unto themselves. They should come beside the local church for a specific task and work toward handing over the baton on a future day.

Related to this option is that such organizations should be evolving on a continual basis. What they do today is not what they should be doing tomorrow. As the Church develops and the contexts change, the parachurch ministries should morph to tackle new matters for the sake of the Kingdom.

Two hundred years of Protestant missionary history have revealed related problems when Western missionaries entered Majority World areas. Though there was cooperation in mind in the beginning, paternalism created codependency. We should have learned our lessons "over there" in cross-cultural contexts, but we have created variations on similar themes "over here" among our own.

Cooperation, not codependency. Partnership in the gospel, not paternalism (Philippians 1:5).

❖ ❖ ❖

Call Your People to Marketable Skills and Degrees

We pastors often forget that stewardship extends beyond the realm of giving money for gospel advancement. For the longest time, we have allowed the notion of being a wise steward to be defined according to money. And while the issue of finances does exist within the jurisdiction of stewardship, stewardship embraces all of the Christian life.

One of the areas we often overlook is recognizing the connection between being a wise steward and career-making decisions. Sadly, we do not consider this matter related to our equipping the saints for the work of the ministry.

Let's let the guidance counselors and career planners shepherd our church members through this massive, life-changing, path-setting decision. We pastors are to be about rightly dividing the Word.

And such a response reveals just how much we have been influenced by secular thought, separating the spiritual from the material.

Pastors, we need to be equipping our parents and their teenagers to make wise Kingdom-advancing decisions when it comes to selecting a college major or obtaining a marketable skill. They need to make such decisions in light of what would best position them in the global market for making disciples and planting churches across North America and the world.

Yes, I know that person in your church wants to study art history and go into $60,000 worth of debt to obtain the coveted B.A. degree. But in light of the global task that is set before us, is that really the path of the wise steward? Maybe it is for that person; maybe the Lord is doing something unusual in that believer's life. However, degrees and skills that generally have little relevance for job placement among the unbelievers and bring haunting debt to that young adult should cause us to consider the stewardship of selecting such paths.

We have neglected to establish within our faith families cultures of expectation that our young people should obtain skills and degrees that would best position them as teams in the marketplaces of the world. Wise decisions made in high school will enable them to support themselves, regularly connect with unbelievers, make disciples, and multiply churches. We have primarily thought that such "real" ministry belongs only to those who are able to get through Bible college and seminary. The irony is that often people with those degrees struggle to find relevant ways to get into the marketplaces and communities of the world. Need I say *platform development*?

I want to challenge you to begin to make the cultural shift within your church. Don't leave one of the most important decisions that a believer will make to the direction of an unbelieving guidance counselor, the whimsical desires of youth, or the materialistic society in which we live.

The Psalmist writes, "May God be gracious to us and bless us and make his face to shine upon us, that your way may be known on earth, your saving power among all nations" (Psalm 67:1-2).

Our Father has blessed members of your congregation with the capabilities to move into the workforce and to go to college. For their own selfish gain? Of course not. Rather, that the way of the Lord may be known among all the nations.

Teach your people that being a wise steward involves prayerfully considering the marketable skills and degrees that would best position them for global disciple making.

❖ ❖ ❖

Stop Trying to Google Your Strategy

I recently came across a word that I did not know, one that was not included in a Webster's dictionary due to its technical use in the field of biology. What was I to do? Google it, of course!

And I had my answer in seconds.

Back in my college days when email was *avant-garde* and I avoided computers like the plague, such instant gratification was not possible.

However, it is a new day. As long as we are wired, we get what we want now.

While expecting instant results is now part of our mindset, it can be problematic for leaders. A culture that demands speed tempers us to push against the fruit of the Spirit, especially in matters of patience and self-control (Galatians

5:22-23). While we could think of numerous practical examples of this, one place where this conflict is found is in the realm of strategic planning. Conflicted expectations here are not good for leaders or the people we lead.

John Mark Terry and I define strategic planning as

a prayerfully discerned, Spirit-guided process, of preparation, development, implementation, and evaluation of the necessary steps involved for missionary endeavors (Developing a Strategy for Missions).

Discerned
Guided
Process
Development
Implementation
Evaluation
Steps

Nothing quick involved. Such is the way of all strategy. Nothing immediate. Strategic planning wars against the instant and our desire to live in the now. You can't Google your strategy.

Every good leader is a strategist. Every good leader bears the fruit of the Spirit. And that includes patience and self-control.

Do you need to grow as a leader by stepping away from your search engine for a while?

Conclusion

This book has been about movement to the edge. However, it is not enough to get there. As I mentioned in the Preface, it is the step beyond that is all-important.

My family and I recently returned from a spring break trip to Washington, DC. We spent the week riding the rails and buses across the city, seeing the sites that the tourists are supposed to see. My favorite stop was the Smithsonian National Air and Space Museum. I have had an interest in astronomy, astronautics, and aeronautics for some time. This museum is filled with stories of men and women who went to the edge and beyond.

I came across this fascinating quote from Charles Lindbergh. These words reveal his reflections on the global impact of his completion of the first transatlantic, non-stop, solo flight (from New York to Paris in 33.5 hours):

> *I was astonished at the effect my successful landing in France had on the nations of the world. To me, it was like a match lighting a bonfire.*

As I reflected on his quote, I could not help but think about what he risked to get to the edge of the boundaries of aviation. And once he took that next step, he changed the world.

History has its share of people who moved beyond the edge. Ferdinand Magellan was the first person to circumnavigate the globe. His act was motivational, for many sailors followed his example. Edmund Hillary and Tenzing Norgay risked their lives to be the first climbers to scale Mt. Everest. After their accomplishment, many climbers would burn with desire to follow in their steps. Across time, multitudes of men and women have been going to the edge of the status quo and one-step beyond.

Most of them took great risks to make great accomplishments and inspire others to make great accomplishments for humanity. Much of the world is in a better place because of their sacrifices. But many of these accomplishments did not make eternal impacts. We may be able to make temporal gains, but apart from Jesus we can do nothing (John 15:5).

While many people of this world are willing to make great sacrifices to move in new directions, I am troubled at times when I reflect on how the Church often responds to the call to make disciples of all nations. Many of us in the West know very little about sacrifice for the Kingdom. And we rarely think in terms of how what we do could be used by the Spirit to encourage, motivate, and inspire others to greater Kingdom labors. We rarely go to the edge. . . and that step beyond seldom comes to mind.

I don't know where the edge is for you, but I hope you get there soon and take that next step. We have incredible potential as Kingdom citizens to advance the gospel among the peoples of this world. The opportunities at home and abroad are numerous. The gospel we have is a message capable of sparking a spontaneous reaction among those who embrace it. It is a message that results in healing and transformation. It tears down strongholds, lifts the broken, and restores that which is damaged beyond human repair.

The first century believers were motivated by a message of great news and were led by an indwelling Spirit. What they did was encouraging and inspiring. Their Kingdom labors served to advance the gospel among those who had never heard it.

Paul went to the edge and took the next step. He knew the gospel was the "power of God for salvation to everyone who believes" (Romans 1:17). And, wow! Those new believers comprising that new church in Thessalonica certainly stepped over the edge:

> For not only has the word of the Lord sounded forth from you in Macedonia and Achaia, but your faith in God has gone forth everywhere, so that we need not say anything (1 Thessalonians 1:8).

So, what are we doing today, by the Holy Spirit's empowerment, to help facilitate the multiplication of disciples, leaders, and churches across the street and across the globe?

Are we intentionally and consistently moving to the edge and beyond that the 4 billion may come to know Him?

Or, are we staying as far from the edge as possible?

Being on the edge means being on the frontiers of Kingdom expansion. Going beyond the edge means you are blazing new directions. You are innovating as the Spirit leads. You are seeing things that few people have seen. However, this comes with risk. Peter, Paul, and the other early believers were not immune to persecution from unbelievers. They also experienced conflict within the Church as they went to the edge and beyond (Acts 11:1-3; 15:1-5).

Evangelicals do have a history of going to the edge and beyond (e.g., the use of radio, agricultural science, medicine, *Jesus* film), but such is not a widespread value among our churches. More Spirit-led innovation is needed for gospel advancement and the multiplication of disciples, leaders, and churches.

What will we risk to get to the edge and beyond?
What will your church risk?
What will your network risk?
What will your mission agency risk?
What will your seminary risk?
What will we risk?
What will I risk?
What will you risk?

What are the characteristics of a Missional church?

Books:
① Charles Brock - Indegenous Church Planting

Made in the USA
Middletown, DE
23 December 2015